greeting cards
in stitches

30 designs

hand-embroidered embellishments

Sharon and Kristin Jankowicz

greeting cards

in stitches

30 designs

hand-embroidered embellishments

Sharon and Kristin Jankowicz

Creative Publishing international

Sharon and Kristin Jankowicz, mother and daughter, design projects for the craft industry. Each a professional graphic designer and versatile needle-crafter, they are a witty, dynamic design duo. Their collaborative fine art, mixed media, altered art pieces, needlework, and craft pieces are sold to private collectors as well as the craft industry, editors, publishers, and manufacturers. Sharon has taught calligraphy to hundreds of students and has worked as a professional calligrapher for over 25 years. That amounts to hand lettering literally thousands of wedding invitations! Kristin majored in graphic design, with a special interest in typography, at both the University of Illinois and at Central St. Martin's College of Art & Design in London, England. Every project created in their Illinois studio has the fingerprints of both all over it.

We dedicate this book to everyone who shares their heart by handcrafting something that brings love and light into the life of another.

To my wonderful husband Jim: "I can never thank you enough for all of the love you fill my life with!"

To my sunshine, sweet Kristi Loo: "You make me happy!!!"

To my family and friends: "Thank you for being so patient and understanding."

Love you, Sharon

Thank you especially to Rhett for your support and patience. "You make all of my days brighter. 'The orange one' and I love you very much."

To you, my 'extended family' in Chicago, "It's a gift to be aware that some of the best years of my life are happening right now. I'll always treasure our time here all together."

"Thank you, Mom and Dad, for being the most encouraging, inspirational, and loving parents imaginable. Dad, you are the ultimate role model and, Mom, I can't think of a single person I'd rather work with. I'm the luckiest daughter in the world."

Love, Kristin

Copyright 2008
Creative Publishing international, Inc.
18705 Lake Drive East
Chanhassen, Minnesota 55317
1-800-328-3895
www.creativepub.com
All rights reserved

Printed in Singapore

10 9 8 7 6 5 4 3 2 1

Library of Congress Cataloging-in-Publication Data
Jankowicz, Sharon.
  Greeting cards in stitches : 30 designs with hand-embroidered embellishments / Sharon Jankowicz, Kristin Jankowicz.
     p. cm.
Includes bibliographical references.
  ISBN-13: 978-1-58923-337-9 (soft cover)
  ISBN-10: 1-58923-337-9 (soft cover)
  1. Greeting cards. 2. Embroidery--Patterns. I. Jankowicz, Kristin.
II. Title.
  TT672.J35 2007
  745.594'1--dc22   2007010468

President/CEO: Ken Fund

Vice President/Sales & Marketing: Peter Ackroyd

Publisher: Winnie Prentiss

Executive Managing Editor: Barbara Harold

Acquisition Editors: Linda Neubauer, Deborah Cannarella

Development Editor: Sharon Boerbon Hanson

Production Managers: Laura Hokkanen, Linda Halls, Stasia Dorn

Creative Director: Michele Lanci-Altomare

Senior Design Manager: Brad Springer

Design Managers: Jon Simpson, Mary Rohl

Director of Photography: Tim Himsel

Lead Photographer: Steve Galvin

Photo Coordinator: Joanne Wawra

Book Design: Mary Rohl

Cover Design: Mary Rohl

Page Layout: Tina R. Johnson

Illustrator: Kristin Jankowicz

Photographer: Andrea Rugg

Creative Writing Assistance: Melony Morris Acosta

contents

boutique chic, tailor-made cards

Personalized cards, embellished with hand stitching, that are so spectacular they'll keep them forever!

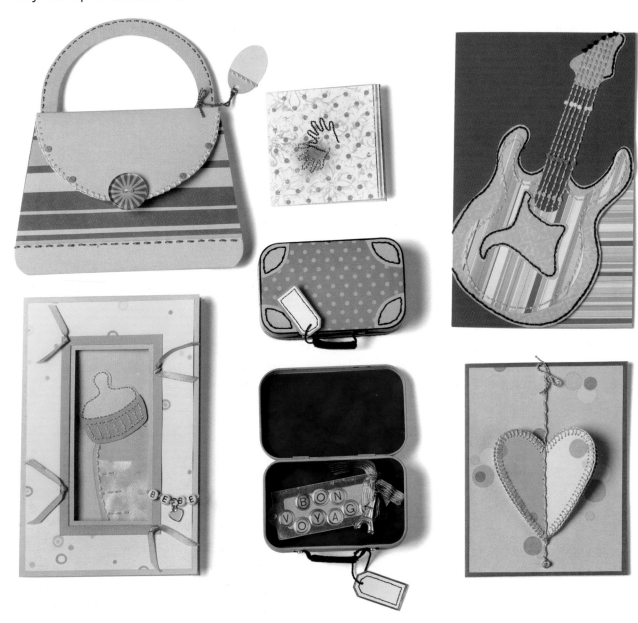

But who really has time for this stuff?

You might be surprised to learn that you do! In the time it takes to get strapped in your car, navigate to the store, hunt through racks for a cat card that resembles "Fluffy" and try to personalize it by writing over parts of the pre-written message, you could

have had some fun, saved some gas, and created the perfect card that will be treasured for years to come.

It's true that these unique gifts take a little more effort—and postage—than the drug store version, but we're sure that you'll never find one in the trash.

For the crafty and the clumsy

Whether you're a seasoned stitcher or you think that the "eye" of a needle has lashes, these projects give a face-lift to traditional needlework—and the stitches are painless!

There are "piercing holes" on our patterns to give you a guide for perfectly spaced stitches. The piercing holes are the holes that the needle will go through when you make your stitches—it's so simple, it brings back fond memories of those nursery school lace-up cards.

We do share the type of stitches that we used to create each card, but you can stitch or ditch what you like. Have a favorite stitch? Don't let us dictate where you use it!

The beauty of this book is in the basics. If you're one of those people who feels more comfortable crafting an exact replica of a project, then we have provided step-by-step instructions, specific product lists, patterns, and complete stitch diagrams just for you. On the other hand, we're realistic. We know that it's more enjoyable—and saves time and money— when you make your own variations and use the stuff you snatched up at the craft store sale and have stashed right there at home.

We don't always like to follow directions (and we don't expect you to, either!).

It's our hope that you'll mold our designs to fit your own personal style. Improvise with different paper prints, color choices, stitches, and embellishments. Just so that you can get an idea of what we're talking about, we've actually worked up different interpretations of each other's projects. The extra suitcase, purses and strip cards are real examples of how each of us had a different way of styling and individualizing the projects. You've got the idea. Amuse yourself and amaze your friends by creating your own versions!

In this book, we'll show you how to make some general types of cards: tags, mini suitcases, peek-a-boo cards, picture frame cards, two-fold cards, and a presentation pocket. We'll even share our secret for the fastest, cutest envelopes ever.

Of course, you'll want to stitch up names and greetings to add to your cards, so we've included some great alphabets and instructions for that too. Once you're ready to roll with the basic techniques, you can make your own variations and mix and match them with any patterns. Want to take it a step further? Try substituting fabric for a piece of the design or use your creations in a scrapbook. You can even put a design onto a gift box, magnet, jewelry pin, or on clothes. You'll have completely original, ultra-personalized embellishments that your friends will envy.

little luggage mint tin suitcases

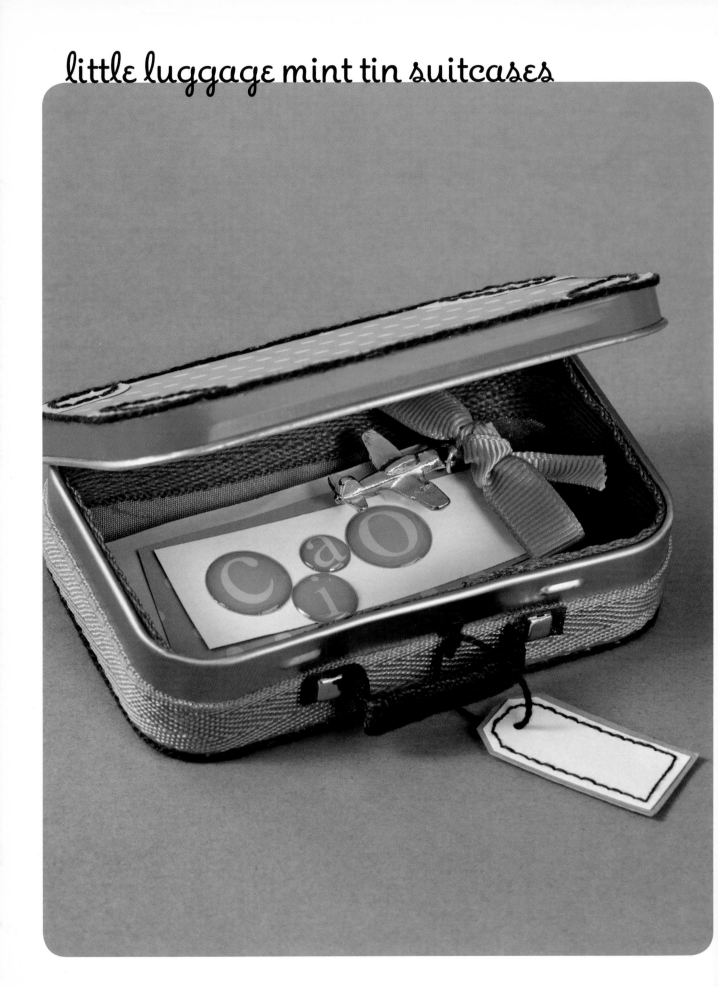

This suitcase was designed with detail in mind, complete with a miniature handle and tiny ID tag. More than a card, it's a thoughtful, custom-made piece of luggage packed with love. Stash a little cash, your photo, or some candy inside. This card is small and durable enough to tuck in a pocket and take along on a trip.

you'll need

tools

transfer tools
ruler
craft scissors
paper piercing tools
self-healing craft mat
mouse pad
embroidery scissors
crewel needles:
    medium and fine
hammer
small nail

materials

glue stick: extra-strength,
    acid-free
cotton embroidery floss:
    very dark blue-violet
clean mint tin
jewel glue
12" (30.5 cm) twill tape:
    turquoise, purple
flat shoelace: black
pearl cotton, size 5: black
two square mini brads: silver
alphabet letters: domed circles
6" (15.2 cm) grosgrain ribbon,
    ⅜" (1 cm) wide: purple
charm, button,
    or other embellishment
adhesive foam squares:
    double-sided

papers & cardstocks

paper: tiny dot print, turquoise
cardstock: white, aqua, purple

step-by-step directions

Refer to the instructions for transferring patterns (page 82) and piercing holes (page 72).

exterior

1. Transfer the pattern (page 87) for the top and bottom suitcase coverings onto the patterned paper. Transfer the corner piece pattern (page 87) eight times onto the turquoise paper. Cut all the pieces out.

2. Glue the corner pieces to the suitcase coverings with a touch of glue stick.

3. Pierce the stitching holes.

4. Thread a medium crewel needle with three strands of the very dark blue-violet embroidery floss. *Double running stitch* (page 76) around each of the eight corner pieces.

5. Adhere the top and bottom suitcase coverings to your mint tin with a thin, even coat of jewel glue. Glue three strands of very dark blue-violet embroidery floss (twisted together) around the perimeter of the suitcase covering paper.

6. Coat one side of the turquoise twill tape with a thin layer of jewel glue. Adhere the tape to the sides of the bottom section of the tin. Trim away any excess.

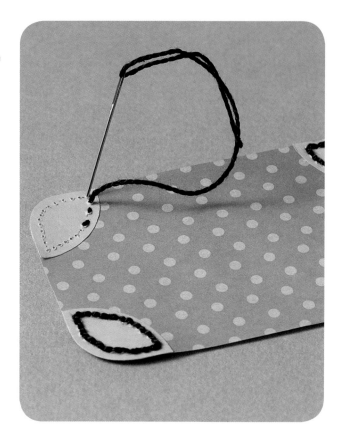

handle

1. Mark a section of shoelace 3" (7.6 cm) long. Run a line of jewel glue across the ends of the shoelace at each mark and allow it to dry. This will keep the shoelace from unraveling. Cut at the marks.

2. Run a thin line of jewel glue onto the middle inch of the shoelace and allow it to dry. Wrap black pearl cotton around the middle section to form the little handle. Secure each end with a drop of glue.

3. Attach the handle just below the lid, using a touch of jewel glue at each end.

4. Close the tin. Pound a nail hole at each end of the handle, through the shoelace, twill tape, and tin. Attach a brad through both holes.

tip

Don't use knots. They will create unwanted lumps under the paper. Instead, tape down the beginning threads and ending tails on the wrong side of the paper.

interior

1. Transfer the pattern for the suitcase linings (page 87) to the solid paper and cut them out. Glue the linings inside the suitcase with glue stick.

2. Coat one side of the purple twill tape with a thin layer of jewel glue. Cover the inside edges of the suitcase bottom with the twill tape. Trim away any excess. This will hide the brad prongs and give the inside of the suitcase a finished look.

3. Layer decreasing sizes of colored cardstock, printed paper, and white cardstock. Attach them to each other with glue stick.

4. Spell out your special message with alphabet letter stickers on the top strip. Decorate the message with ribbon tied into a bow and a charm—or add a trim, buttons, or whatever strikes your fancy.

5. Adhere the message inside the suitcase with double-sided adhesive foam squares for extra dimension.

tiny tag

1. Transfer the tiny tag patterns (page 87) to the purple and white cardstocks and cut them out.

2. Pierce the stitching holes into the white tag. *Double running stitch* around the white tag using a single strand of embroidery floss in the fine crewel needle.

3. Center the white tag, right side up, on the purple tag and glue them together with glue stick.

4. Pierce a hole at the top center of the tag. Thread black pearl thread into the hole, and tie your ID tag onto the suitcase handle. Write the name of the traveler, their destination, or something important like, "love U," in itsy-bitsy handwriting on this tiny tag. Now it's "good to go!"

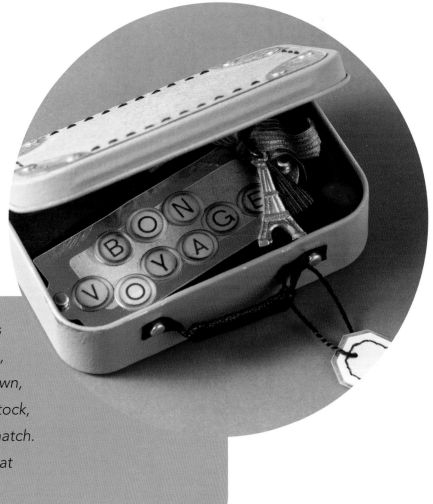

style option:

Here's another luggage style that's suitable for guys. For this variation, the mint tin was spray painted brown, then finished off with paper, cardstock, and embellishments in colors to match. The message was arranged on a flat metallic label frame.

polka-dot petals

This "loopy" version of a classic daisy makes a hip way to say hello. Choose your favorite colors to make the card more personal or match it to wrapping paper or a gift bag for an especially thoughtful tag. This design is easy enough for even the greenest embroiderers. Keep it simple or stitch yourself a whole bouquet of these funky flowers.

step-by-step directions

Refer to the instructions for transferring patterns (page 82), scoring (page 66), and piercing holes (page 72).

1. Cut a 4" x 8" (10.2 x 20.3 cm) rectangle from the dot paper. Score the back of the paper along the halfway point. Fold the paper in half to crease. Then lay it flat.

2. Transfer the circle pattern (page 87) onto a piece of gold cardstock. Cut out the circle and adhere it to the front, center of the card, using just a touch of glue stick. This will hold the circle in place, but you won't have to sew through anything sticky.

3. Transfer the daisy pattern over the gold circle. Pierce holes at all the marked dots.

4. *Running stitch* (page 76) with white pearl cotton around the large outer circle.

5. *Double running stitch* (page 76) blue pearl cotton around the petals. Viola! Your cute flower card is ready to brighten someone's day.

you'll need

tools

transfer tools
ruler
craft scissors
paper piercing tools
self-healing craft mat
mouse pad
bone folder
embroidery scissors
chenille needle: size 22

materials

glue stick: extra-strength, acid-free
pearl cotton, size 5: white, royal blue

papers & cardstocks

paper: polka-dot print
cardstock: gold

hands in harmony mini card

Less is more with this precious little card. The symbolism of the two hands is universal, while the simplicity and peaceful palette perfectly match the sweet sentiment that goes into a hand-stitched creation. The miniature stitches in this design make it slightly more delicate than most, so be sure to put as much care into the stitching as you put into choosing the lucky recipient. No matter what the occasion, you can easily adapt this card to suit it—change the color of the hands, add jeweled rings or wedding bands, or even try sewing a pretty mini-ruffle around the wrists to make a tiny pair of gloves.

step-by-step directions

Refer to the instructions for transferring patterns (page 82), scoring (page 66), and piercing holes (page 72).

1. Cut a 3" x 6" (7.6 x 15.2 cm) rectangle from the brocade dot paper. Score the back of the paper along the halfway point. Fold the paper in half to crease it. Then lay it flat.

2. Transfer the small hands pattern (page 89) onto the front, center of the card.

3. With your finger, lightly rub a small amount of the wax finish over the hand on the left.

4. Thread the needle with three strands of silver embroidery floss and carefully *double running stitch* (page 76) around the hand on the left.

5. Carefully *double running stitch* the second hand with three strands of green embroidery floss.

6. Cut a narrow strip from the striped paper. Glue it on the bottom of the card. Trim any excess hanging over the edges with craft scissors.

you'll need

○ tools

transfer tools
ruler
craft scissors
paper piercing tools
self-healing craft mat
mouse pad
bone folder
embroidery scissors
crewel needle: fine

○ materials

wax metallic finish: turquoise
metallic embroidery floss:
    silver
cotton embroidery floss:
    sage green
glue stick: extra-strength,
    acid-free

○ papers

paper: brocade dot print,
    stripe

boho paisley motif

"If it ain't broke, don't fix it." That was our inspiration for this pretty paisley. It's classic and still stylish as ever, so we didn't mess with a good thing. A few simple stitches are all it takes to accentuate the design. The paper doesn't even have to match perfectly (it's actually better if it doesn't), so it's effortless to make beautiful, unique cards.

step-by-step directions

Refer to the instructions for transferring patterns (page 82), scoring (page 66), and piercing holes (page 72).

1. Cut an 8" x 7¾" (20.3 x 19.7 cm) rectangle from pink paper. On the back, measure 4" (10.2 cm) from one edge and score. When folded, the back will stick out ½" (1.3 cm) from the front of the card. Fold the paper along the score line to crease. Then lay it flat.

2. Cut a 1" x 7¾" (2.5 x 19.7 cm) strip of paisley paper. Glue it, face up, to the underside of the card front, making both edges line up. Both sides of the card will be the same width.

3. Cut a 3" x 4" (7.6 x 10.2 cm) rectangle out of the brown paper. Glue it toward the top of the front of the card, centered on the pink paper.

4. Cut out a paisley motif from the paisley paper. Glue it at the bottom left of the rectangle, with a bit extending off of the brown paper at the side and bottom.

5. Pierce stitching holes down the right joint, where the light pink and paisley papers meet. Also pierce holes around the inside of the brown tweed rectangle and along the curves of the large paisley motif.

6. *Backstitch* (page 80) down the right joint, where the light pink and paisley papers meet, with brown pearl cotton. Then make a blue *French knot* (page 78) at every third stitch.

7. Still using the blue pearl cotton, add several *French knots* on the inside of the large paisley motif and *backstitch* to embellish the bottom detail.

8. Using pink pearl cotton, *stem stitch* (page 81) around the inside of the brown tweed rectangle. Then add *French knots* along the middle of the large paisley motif and *straight stitch* (page 75) along the upper curve.

you'll need

tools

transfer tools
ruler
craft scissors
paper piercing tools
self-healing craft mat
mouse pad
bone folder
embroidery scissors
chenille needle: size 22

materials

glue stick: extra-strength, acid-free
pearl cotton, size 5: bright blue, pink, brown

papers

papers: light pink print, brown tweed print, paisley print

savvy stitched strips

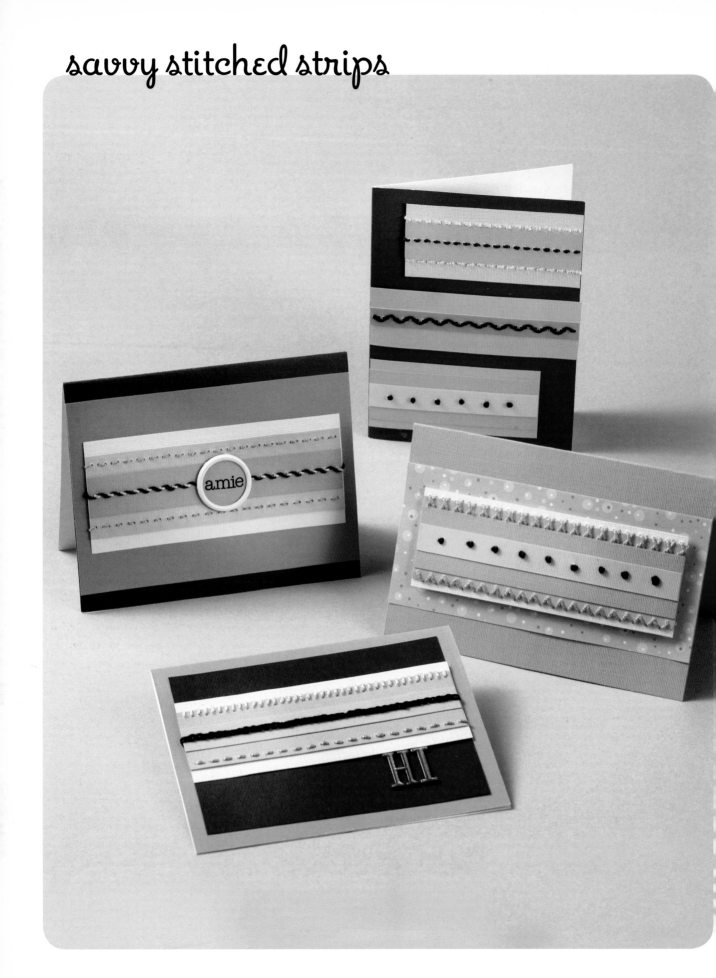

When time or supplies run short, whip up one of these clever strip cards using scraps of cardstock, paper, or even fabric. This will be one of your most used card ideas because it lets you use all of those little bits and pieces that you've been hanging on to. Admit it, you save those little bits, don't you? Just don't tell anyone that you made this very special card out of leftovers!

Layer strips of cardstock and paper; then add a line or two or three of your favorite stitches. Add charms, letters, or doodads—whatever you happen to have on hand—for a professional, finished look.

We stitched up several samples so that you can see just a few of the unlimited possibilities. WARNING: making these quickie cards can be addictive.

tip

- **stitching through adhesive**
  stuck on you... Glue stick is the best adhesive for attaching layers that you're going to stitch through. It dries and doesn't stay sticky, like many other adhesives. Sticky adhesives will gum up your needle, making it harder to stitch and sometimes making a mess.

- **paper crumples**
  get tough... Paper often tears and crumples easily during stitching. Solve that problem by making the paper stronger. Reinforce your paper by adhering it to cardstock with glue stick adhesive.

- **starting and ending a stitch**
  tape tails and don't get tied up... When making cards, you don't want to use knots because they'll create a bump through the paper or cardstock. Instead, secure the beginning and ending tails of thread on the back of your stitching surface with tape.

you'll need

tools
transfer tools
ruler
pencil & eraser
craft scissors
paper piercing tools
self-healing craft mat
mouse pad
bone folder
embroidery scissors
chenille needle: size 22

materials
glue stick: extra-strength,
    acid-free
pearl cotton, size 5:
    assorted colors
double-sided tape
adhesive foam squares:
    double-sided
embellishments:
    white circle frame, metal
    letters, rub-on letters
premade blank card & envelope

papers & cardstocks
paper: pink dot print
textured cardstock:
    assorted colors

Note: Follow the manufacturer's
    instructions to attach
    embellishments to your card.

◯step-by-step directions

Refer to the instructions for piercing holes (page 72) and scoring (page 66).

general construction

1. Play with different arrangements of cardstock and paper strips until you find a combination and layout that looks great to you.
2. Use a glue stick to adhere the strips together.
3. Use a ruler and pencil to mark stitching holes for the chosen stitchwork. Pierce holes in the paper pieces as needed. Erase the pencil marks.
4. Thread the needle with pearl cotton and stitch to your heart's desire.
5. Adhere the stitched strips to your card with a glue stick, double-sided tacky tape, or double-sided adhesive foam squares.

just peachy card

1. Glue a patterned strip across a greeting card.
2. Layer, then glue together, cardstock of two different colors and widths. *Straight stitch* in a *zigzag* (page 75) pattern across the bottom and *cross stitch* (page 75) pattern across the top. Adhere the sewn strip to the center of the patterned strip with foam squares.
3. Layer, then glue together, cardstock of two different colors and widths. The largest should be narrow enough to fit within the first layer. Make *French knots* (page 78) across the strip with contrasting embroidery floss. Glue to the first layer.

"hi" card

1. Glue a brown strip to a greeting card, leaving a border.
2. Layer, then glue together, cardstock of two different colors and widths. *Straight stitch* across the top and *running stitch* (page 76) across the bottom. Glue to the center of the brown strip.
3. *Chain stitch* (page 77) across a narrow strip. Glue to the other layer.
4. Adhere the metal letters.

style options:

Make impressive place cards by using a smaller version of the blue & pink name card. Use the extra space at the bottom of the mocha & kiwi "HI" card to spell out "Get Well," "Thanks," or whatever message you'd like to send. Try some trendy metal embellishment letters. Play with various arrangements of cardstock and paper strips until you find the paper combination and layout that looks great to you. Choose a color of pearl cotton that enhances your composition and paper colors.

tip

A glue stick allows a little "wiggle time" before it dries so that you can position your strips exactly the way you'd like them.

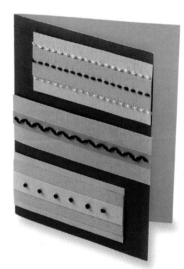

name frame card

1. Glue a wide blue strip to a greeting card.

2. Layer, then glue together cardstock of two different colors and widths. *Running stitch* across the top and bottom. Glue to the blue strip.

3. *Whipped running stitch* (page 77) across a strip using two colors of embroidery floss. Glue to the other layer.

4. Create a message or name with rub-on letters on cardstock. Place the message in a circle frame and trim the paper. Adhere the frame to the center of the stacked strips.

three-strip card

1. Layer, then glue together, cardstock of three different colors and widths. *French knot* along the center. Glue the stack to the lower left of a brown greeting card.

2. Layer, then glue together, cardstock of two different colors and widths. *Whipped running stitch* across the top. Glue the stack in the middle of the card.

3. Layer, then glue together, cardstock of two different colors and widths. *Running stitch* across the center and *straight stitch* along the edges of the top strip. Glue the stack to the upper right of the card.

guitar greetings

Guitars are all the rage and your cutting-edge card will be, too. Whether you know someone who loves music or who is into the latest icons, they'll love this version of the classic six-string. Feel free to make the guitar as fancy as you like with rhinestones, wild paper, or even metallic floss. Rock on, baby!

step-by-step directions

Refer to the instructions for transferring patterns (page 82), scoring (page 66), and piercing holes (page 72).

1. Transfer the guitar base, center and handle patterns (page 88) onto turquoise paper. Transfer the guitar stem pattern onto burgundy cardstock, and transfer the inner guitar base pattern onto striped paper.

2. Cut the cardstock into a 9" x 7½" (22.9 x 19.1 cm) rectangle. Score the back of the paper along the halfway point. Fold the paper in half.

3. Use a glue stick to assemble the guitar pieces. Then, slant the entire guitar to the right and glue it to the front of the card (refer to photo).

4. Open the card. Pierce holes along the pattern lines, ⅛" (3 mm) from the edge.

5. *Backstitch* (page 80) around the striped paper inner base and down the strings with yellow pearl cotton.

6. From the bottom to the top, make a row of yellow *French knots* (page 78), blue-violet *French knots,* white *French knots,* and then black *French knots* at even increments up the stem of the guitar.

7. Using black pearl cotton, *backstitch* around the turquoise base and center, as well as down the right side of the handle.

8. Cut away the burgundy cardstock along the bottom right edge of the guitar.

9. Cut a 4½" (11.4 cm) square piece of striped paper. Glue it along the bottom of the inside of the card.

you'll need

○ tools

transfer tools
ruler
craft scissors
paper piercing tools
self-healing craft mat
mouse pad
bone folder
embroidery scissors
chenille needle: size 22

○ materials

glue stick: extra-strength, acid-free
pearl cotton, size 5: yellow, white, blue-violet, black

○ papers & cardstocks

papers: turquoise print, striped print
cardstock: burgundy

This card is just as hip as a real flip phone but speaks volumes more, and there is no more fun way to drop a line to a special friend. There's a whole lot of stitching that you can do on this card, but you can also make it simpler by leaving out some details (especially on the inside!). Write a note on the inside screen or paste a picture there and replace the buttons at the bottom with your message. R-I-N-G... it's for you!

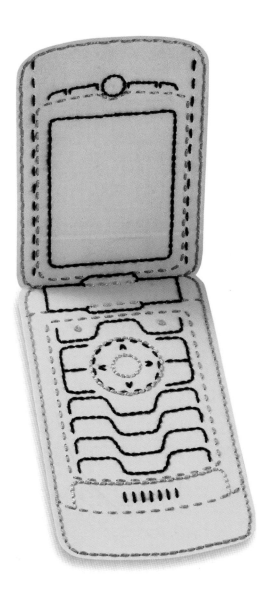

you'll need

⃝ tools

transfer tools
ruler
craft shears
paper piercing tools
self-healing craft mat
mouse pad
bone folder
embroidery scissors
tapestry needle: size 22

⃝ materials

pearl cotton, size 5:
    black, light pink,
    dark pink, violet
double-sided tape
jewel glue

⃝ cardstocks

cardstock: light pink,
    dark pink, violet

step-by-step directions

Refer to the instructions for piercing holes (page 72).

inside

1. Transfer the entire inside pattern (page 91) onto light pink cardstock.

2. Pierce the stitching holes on the inside pattern. Do not punch holes on the base yet.

3. *Backstitch* (page 80) with black pearl cotton around the "buttons," the speaker slits, the middle joint, the screen, and the details at the top center. *Running stitch* (page 76) around the inner dial circle and the direction arrows.

4. *Running stitch* with dark pink pearl cotton around the top screen and bottom buttons and under the speaker slits.

5. *Running stitch* with violet pearl cotton in the center of the middle joint. *Backstitch* around the outer line of the dial, the innermost circle, and the bottom detail around the speaker slits. Add *French knots* (page 78) in the center of each top button.

6. Use the bone folder to score the violet card stock and fold it in half. Also fold stitched cell in half along the top of the middle joint (refer to photo on page 25).

7. Apply double-sided tape in a few places along the backside of the stitched cell phone. Without allowing

the two pieces of cardstock to stick, carefully align the folds, leaving a gap of about 1⁄16" (1.6 mm) between the two papers; then place the folded cell sheet inside the folded violet sheet and adhere them together. This will allow the card to close completely and will also allow it to open at about a 90 degree angle. Do not open the card more than 90 degrees once you have completed step 12.

8. Place a mouse pad facedown on your work surface and poke holes around the outline of the cell pattern, through both sheets of cardstock.

9. Cut a 55" (140 cm) strand of dark pink pearl cotton. Then tie a knot at the end, leaving a 2" (5.1 cm) tail. From the back, poke the threaded needle through the fold at the center left of the middle joint. The knot will be sticking out of the top of the folded card.

10. *Backstitch* around the bottom outline of the cell phone. Stop when you get back to the fold at the center right of the middle joint, and tie a knot leaving a 2" (5.1 cm) tail. This knot will also stick out of the fold.

11. Cut a 40" (101.6 cm) strand of dark pink pearl cotton. Tie it to the 2" (5.1 cm) tail. Do not snip the two tails off.

12. From the outside, *running stitch* around the top outline of the cell phone. Then, turn around and *running stitch* back to the starting point. Tie this piece of pearl cotton to the two tails. Snip them all as short as possible.

front

1. Transfer the cell phone front pattern (page 91) onto dark pink cardstock. Cut out the front of the cell phone and the center window.

2. Pierce holes following the pattern. Do not pierce the black stitching line down both sides.

3. *Backstitch* with black pearl cotton around the top center circle and window.

4. *Running stitch* with violet along the top of the cell pattern, along the side buttons, and around the bottom circle.

5. *Backstitch* with light pink pearl cotton the top square and the bottom heart.

6. Apply several pieces of double-sided tape on the back at the top and bottom. Line up the front piece on the folded violet cardstock so it fits inside the dark pink stitches, and press firmly.

7. Open the cell phone. Place a mouse pad at the edge of the table and lay the cell phone facedown on the pad, with the bottom half hanging off the edge (this will allow you to pierce holes without straining the paper and the stitches). Pierce stitching holes along the dashed lines—down both sides of the front—through all three pieces of cardstock.

8. Cut a 10" (25.4 cm) piece of black pearl cotton and tie a knot at one end. Starting from the outside top, *running stitch* down one side of the phone. Tie it off with a knot at the outside bottom. Repeat down the other side.

9. With the card closed, use scissors to cut as close as possible (about ⅛" [3 mm]) around the entire perimeter of all pieces of the cell phone. Open the card and finish cutting out the top of the cell phone.

tip When you're closely snipping off tails of knots, put a dab of clear-drying glue on the knot to make sure it doesn't unravel later.

pop-up heart

Someone will know that they're loved when this keepsake card with folded hearts, held together by a single line of stitching, arrives. There's room to rubberstamp a name or a few words onto the exterior folded hearts, then express your innermost feelings over the shadow heart waiting inside.

step-by-step directions

Refer to the instructions for transferring patterns (page 82), scoring (page 66), and piercing holes (page 72).

1. Transfer the heart pattern (page 91) onto the pink dot paper once and onto the bubblegum pink paper three times. Cut out using the craft shears.

2. With a paper trimmer, trim the dot print paper and the apricot cardstock ⅛" (3 mm) smaller on all sides than your card.

3. Apply tape runner adhesive to the wrong side of the dot print paper; then mount it onto the card front. Apply tape runner adhesive to the wrong side of the apricot cardstock; then mount it onto the inside of the card.

4. Apply tape runner adhesive to the wrong side of one solid pink heart. Mount it onto the apricot cardstock inside the card.

5. Score the centers of the remaining paper hearts with a bone folder. Fold each in half.

6. Apply glue stick to the wrong side of the dot print heart. Adhere one folded pink heart under the right half of the dot heart. Adhere the other folded pink heart under the left half of the dot heart. Check out the photo to be sure that you have the hearts in the right order.

7. Trim away any uneven edges; then pierce the stitching holes through all the layers.

8. *Blanket stitch* (page 79) around the edges of the hearts with very light sky blue pearl cotton.

9. Draw a straight line vertically down the center of the front of the card. Apply glue stick to the wrong side of the assembled hearts, align the centers, and mount the assembled hearts onto your card.

10. Open the card and pierce stitching holes along the center line. *Running stitch* (page 76) along the center line with very light sky blue pearl cotton.

11. Starting at the top, weave bubblegum pink pearl cotton through your running stitches, creating a *whipped running stitch* (page 77). At the bottom, tie a knot; then continue weaving a *whipped running stitch* back up to the top of the pattern line. Finish off by tying a tight little bow. Apply a tiny dot of jewel glue to the bow to keep it from untying.

12. Cut out a few dots from a scrap of your dot paper and use glue stick to adhere them to the inside of the card.

you'll need

tools

transfer tools
ruler
pencil
paper trimmer
craft shears
paper piercing tools
self-healing craft mat
mouse pad
bone folder
embroidery scissors
tapestry needle: size 22

materials

premade card & envelope: lavender
tape runner adhesive
glue stick: extra-strength, acid-free
pearl cotton, size 5: very light sky blue, bubblegum pink
jewel glue

papers & cardstocks

papers: pink dot print, bubblegum pink
cardstock: apricot

tip

For a clean, professional look, hide the tails of your thread between the layers of cardstock and paper hearts.

cake!

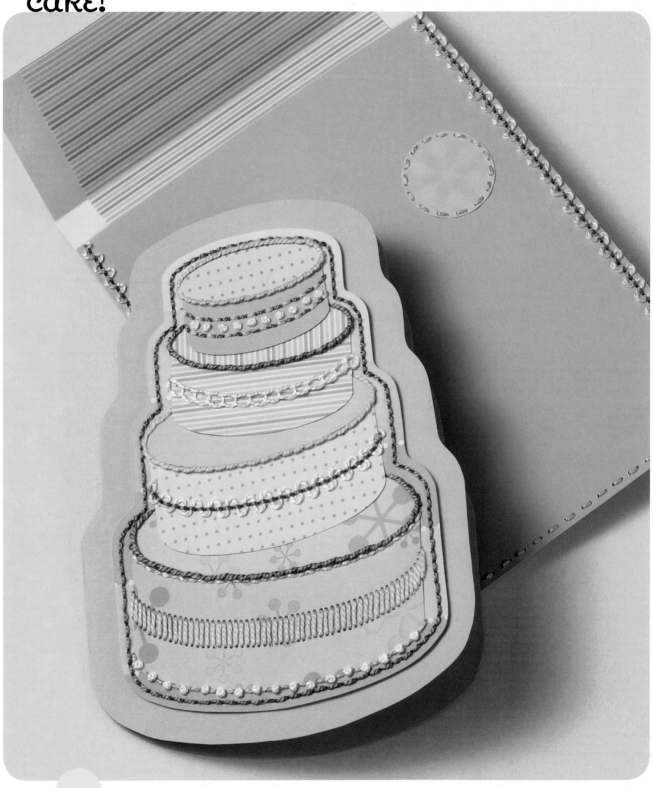

The stitches are the icing on this party pastry. Not only is it a fun way to practice your stitches, but the end result is a confection perfect for tons of different occasions. Add any embellishment as a topper to make it even more personalized. Best of all, it looks extravagant—only you have to know that it's easy as pie!

step-by-step directions

Refer to the instructions for transferring patterns (page 82), scoring (page 66), and piercing holes (page 72).

general assembly

1. Transfer each of the four layers of cake and base (pages 89-90) onto a different piece of patterned paper. We used a different piece—or rotated the same piece—of paper for the top of each tier, but that's just "icing."
2. Cut out all the pieces and glue them into place on the base, starting at the bottom and working your way up.
3. Once assembled, pierce the stitching holes along the pattern lines.

top layer

1. *Stem stitch* (page 81) with gold pearl cotton around the top.
2. Alternate two rows of gold and blue pearl cotton *running stitches* (page 76) across the middle.
3. Make a row of white pearl cotton *French knots* (page 78) between the running stitches.

second layer

1. *Stem stitch* with blue pearl cotton around the top.
2. *Square chain stitch* (page 78) with white pearl cotton across the middle.

third layer

1. *Stem stitch* with gold pearl cotton around the top.
2. *Backstitch* (page 80) with blue pearl cotton across the middle.
3. *Whip backstitch* (page 80) with white pearl cotton.

bottom layer

1. *Stem stitch* with blue pearl cotton around the top.
2. Alternate gold and white pearl cotton *running stitches* under the stem stitch.
3. With gold pearl cotton make a row of vertical *straight stitches* (page 75) across the middle.
4. *Running stitch* with gold pearl cotton along the bottom. Add a white pearl cotton *French knot* between each stitch.

you'll need

tools

transfer tools
craft scissors
paper piercing tools
self-healing craft mat
mouse pad
embroidery scissors
chenille needle: size 22

materials

glue stick: extra-strength, acid-free
pearl cotton, size 5: gold, blue, white

papers & cardstocks

papers: blue dot print, thin striped print, asterisk print, thick striped print
cardstock: light blue

base

1. Outline the cake base with blue pearl cotton *backstitches*.

finishing touches

1. Fold a 10" x 7" (25.4 x 17.8 cm) piece of blue cardstock in half to make a 5" x 7" (12.7 x 17.8 cm) card. Align the card pattern (page 90) and transfer it onto the cardstock (the dotted line down the left side of the pattern signifies the fold of the card).
2. Cut the light blue cardstock card into the shape of the cake. Be sure not to cut the fold!

fuzzy flying heart, tag & pocket

This fuzzy, flying felt heart is the perfect courier to dispatch warm wishes to your sweetie. Glue it to a tag and speed a greeting to someone special, or turn it into a cute pin by attaching a latching pin-back. You can even use the heart as an appliqué. Just use fabric glue to attach it to jeans, a baby onesie, a T-shirt, or even glue the heart onto a book cover or lunch box. The possibilities are endless!

step-by-step directions

Refer to the instructions for transferring patterns (page 82).

felt heart

1. Transfer the wing and heart pattern (page 92) onto a 6" (15.2 cm) piece of sky blue felt. Mount the felt in your embroidery hoop.

2. Use the chenille needle and sky blue pearl cotton to *double running stitch* (page 76) the feathers on the wings. Remove the felt from the hoop and carefully cut out the design.

3. Transfer the large heart pattern onto strawberry felt and the small heart pattern onto sugar plum felt. Cut out the hearts with fabric shears.

4. Position the larger heart over the wing pattern. Use strawberry pearl cotton to *blanket stitch* (page 79) around the outside edge of the heart, catching the layer underneath.

5. Position the small heart on top of the large heart. Use strawberry pearl cotton to *backstitch* (page 80) along the pattern line through both hearts. Use the tapestry needle and lemon pearl cotton to weave under your backstitches, creating *woven backstitches* (page 80).

6. Attach the embellishment with stitches or jewel glue.

you'll need
[for the heart]

tools

transfer tools
fabric shears
embroidery scissors
chenille needle: size 22
tapestry needle: size 22
5" (12.7 cm) embroidery hoop

materials

felt: strawberry, sky blue,
sugar plum
pearl cotton, size 5: sky blue,
strawberry, lemon
bead, button,
or charm embellishment
jewel glue (optional)

○ tools

transfer tools
paper trimmer
craft shears
bone folder
hole punches: ¹⁄₁₆" (1.6 mm),
    ¹⁄₈" (3 mm)

○ materials

glue stick: extra-strength,
    acid-free
6" (15.2 cm) ribbon, ¹⁄₄"
    (6 mm) wide: soft pink
two mini brads: soft pink

○ papers & cardstocks

papers:
    pink dot print,
    1" x 2" (2.5 x 5.1 cm)
cardstock: yellow dot print
textured cardstock: lilac,
    peachy pink

versatile tag

1. Transfer the patterns (page 92) onto the paper and cardstock. Use the paper trimmer to trim along the straight pattern lines. Use craft shears to cut the ¹⁄₂" (1.3 cm) diameter circle of peachy pink cardstock. Use the photo below as a guide.

2. Adhere the yellow dot print cardstock to the lilac cardstock with glue stick.

3. Score the fold line on the pink dot paper with a bone folder; then fold it over the tag and secure on the front and back with glue stick.

4. Punch a ¹⁄₈" (3 mm) hole through the center of the cardstock circle, apply glue stick to the back, then attach it to the center of the pink dot paper square. Now punch a ¹⁄₈" (3 mm) hole through all of the layers of paper and cardstock so that you can lace your ribbon through them.

5. Tie the soft pink ribbon onto the top of the tag.

6. Use the bone folder to score the fold lines on the upper corners of the tag. Fold the corners over and punch a tiny hole for the mini brads to go through. Attach the mini brads.

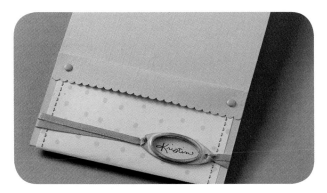

presentation pocket

1. Soften the look of the metal label holder by spraying it with a coat or two of whitewash spray paint. Set it aside to dry while you work on the other parts of the project.

2. Transfer the pocket base pattern (page 93) onto the cardstock and the pocket lining onto the paper. Use the paper trimmer to trim along the straight pattern lines. Cut the scalloped edge of the base with the craft scissors.

3. Score the fold lines with the bone folder; then fold. Apply glue stick to the wrong side of the pink dot print paper and adhere it to the cardstock.

4. Pierce holes for the stitching through all layers of the paper and the cardstock. Thread the tapestry needle with two strands of bubble gum pink embroidery floss. Secure the tails of your thread with a small piece of tape on the inside of the presentation pocket near the stitching line. *Running stitch* (page 76) along each side. Hide the thread tails in the inside of the pocket and secure them with tape.

5. Punch 1/16" (1.66 mm) holes for the mini brads to go through and attach them.

6. Trace the inside and outside of the label holder onto a 1" x 2" (2.5 x 5.1 cm) piece of peachy pink cardstock with a pencil. Write out a name or word on the cardstock with a pen. Use craft shears to cut the cardstock into the shape of your label holder, but slightly smaller, so that it won't show around the edges of the label holder. Erase the pencil marks. Adhere the cardstock to your label holder with jewel glue.

7. Pierce holes through the cardstock beneath the openings on each side of the label holder.

8. Lace the ribbon through the openings on each side of the label holder. Tie the ribbon onto the presentation pocket. Secure the ribbon on the backside of the presentation pocket with a few drops of jewel glue.

you'll need
[presentation pocket]

○ tools

transfer tools
pencil
pen
eraser
paper trimmer
scalloped-edge craft scissors
craft shears
paper piercing tools
self-healing craft mat
mouse pad
bone folder
embroidery scissors
tapestry needle: size 8
hole punch: 1/16" (1.6 mm)

○ materials

whitewash spray paint
metal label holder
glue stick: extra-strength,
    acid-free
cotton embroidery floss:
    bubble gum pink
tape
two mini brads: soft pink
jewel glue
18" (45.7 cm) ribbon,
    3/8" (1 cm) wide:
    bubble gum pink

○ papers & cardstocks

paper: pink dot print
textured cardstock:
    peachy pink

boutique chic purses

It's in the bag … a handy little coordinating pocket to store cash, a gift card; or a little message, that is. These perky purses are a stylish gift for the girls. Design a bag with your own custom colors and embellishments. Wouldn't a patent leather or mock-croc purse knock her right off her high heels? Dangles and "bling" are high fashion, so break out the flowers, ribbons, charms, beads and crystals. And don't forget to personalize with a matching petite tag. Pick a letter from one of the alphabets (pages 85–86) to stitch a monogram on the little tag.

step-by-step directions

Refer to the instructions for transferring patterns (page 82), scoring (page 66), and piercing holes (page 72).

general construction

1. Transfer the patterns (pages 94–95) onto the paper and cardstock. Use craft shears to cut out the pieces.

2. Be sure to cut *two* handles. Apply glue stick to the wrong side of one of the handles. Attach the flat (not the front textured sides) wrong sides of the handles together. Let the glue dry. Pierce the stitching holes through both layers of cardstock along the edge of the handle. Select a stitch and thread; then stitch along the handle edge.

3. Score and crease the cardstock purse. Apply glue stick to the wrong side of the bottom and adhere the printed paper purse front panel. Pierce the stitching holes for the straight line of stitches along the bottom of the purse. Select a stitch and thread; then stitch along the straight line at the bottom of the purse.

4. For now, just pierce the stitching holes along the *top of the pocket only*. Select a stitch, thread, and thread color; then stitch along the straight line at the top of the pocket only.

   Next, apply glue stick to the wrong side of the cardstock pocket, along the edges of the sides and bottom. Adhere the pocket to the right (front) side of the printed paper lining.

   Pierce the stitching holes through the printed paper lining and cardstock pocket for the stitching lines at the sides and bottom of the pocket. Select a stitch and thread; then stitch along the sides and bottom of the pocket.

   OR save some time …

   Skip the hole piercing and stitching. Just adhere the pocket to the lining with double-sided tape applied along the sides and bottom of the pocket.

5. Punch holes through the handle and the cardstock back of the purse outside. Attach brads, snaps, or the fastener of your choice. (For the tiny buttons, don't pierce holes! Adhere the handles to the back of the purse with double-sided tape. Then attach the tiny buttons with mini glue dots.)

6. Score and fold the printed paper lining. Lightly apply glue stick to the wrong side of the paper lining. Position the paper lining into the outside of the purse and lightly smooth it down. Fold the purse as if closing it.

you'll need
[for the general construction]

tools

transfer tools
craft shears
paper piercing tools
self-healing craft mat
mouse pad
bone folder
embroidery scissors
chenille needle: size 22
tapestry needle: size 22
crewel embroidery needle: fine
hole punch: 1/16" (1.6 mm)

materials

glue stick: extra-strength,
    acid-free
pearl cotton, size 5:
    assorted colors
double-sided tape (optional)
mini brads
snap-on metal fasteners
round self-adhesive
    Velcro fasteners
mini glue dots
jewel glue

papers & cardstocks

paper: stripe, chocolate
    flower & paisley print,
    dot print paper
textured cardstock:
    strawberry, sky blue

7. Open the purse and lay it with the cardstock front flap facing up onto your mouse pad.

Fold the handle back out of your way. Pierce the stitching holes through the cardstock flap and paper lining around the edge of the front flap. Select a stitch and thread then stitch around the edge of the front flap.

Attach a Velcro fastener to the inside center of the flap if desired.

8. Embellish! Attach embellishments according to the manufacturer's instructions. We used jewel glue to adhere the beads and mini glue dots to attach the buttons.

buttons & beads bag

1. Apply jewel glue to the back of a clear button. Position the button over a design on your paper. Smooth out any bubbles. Let the glue dry; then trim away the excess paper. Tie a strand of pearl cotton through the button holes. Use double-sided tape to secure the thread tails on the back of the button. Adhere the button to the purse flap with double-sided tape.

2. Transfer your letter pattern onto the bottom of the oval. Pierce tiny stitching holes for your letter. Stitch the letter with two strands of embroidery floss. Apply glue stick to the wrong side of the pink top piece and attach it to the top of the oval. Pierce the stitching holes through both layers. Select thread and do a *running stitch* (page 76) across the tag.

If you'd like to cover the stitching on the back of the tag:

Cut out another oval. Punch a hole at the top and glue the wrong sides of the ovals together. Lace a strand of pearl cotton or ribbon through the hole. Tie the tag to your purse handle.

spring bling flowers bag

1. This purse has lacing all along the sides and across the front. Insert your needle from the back of each stitching hole, pull the thread through to the front, and repeat.

2. Tie the ribbon to the handle.

3. Remove the centers from a few of the flowers and use jewel glue to attach crystal centers. Glue the flowers to the ribbon.

4. Apply the small crystals over the dots printed on the paper with a Creative Crystal, "BeJeweler" Stone Styler, or use tiny dots of jewel glue.

heavy metal bag

1. Apply the round nailheads with a Creative Crystal BeJeweler Stone Styler, or use tiny dots of jewel glue.

2. Add the keychain with charms to the handle.

bébé bottle picture frame card

A picture frame card is a staple for card makers. You'll discover that you can use this picture frame style card as the foundation for all kinds of unique cards. Substitute a different design and add embellishments that match your new colors and theme for a totally custom-made card.

The sturdy layers of cardstock make this card a functional frame for a photo, too.

step-by-step directions

bébé bottle

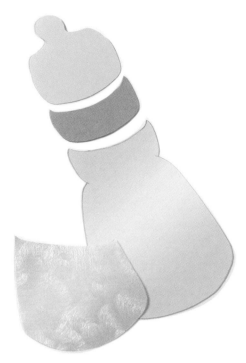

you'll need
[for bébé bottle]

○ tools

transfer tools
craft shears
paper piercing tools
self-healing craft mat
mouse pad
embroidery scissors
crewel embroidery
    needle: medium

○ materials

tracing paper
lightweight vinyl: clear
removable tape
cotton embroidery floss:
    very light baby blue,
    bright pink, light lavender
glue stick: extra-strength,
    acid-free

○ papers & cardstocks

textured paper: white
cardstock: light pink, lavender

1. Transfer the bottle (vinyl) pattern (page 96) onto tracing paper. Lay the tracing paper on top of the clear plastic and secure it in position with removable tape. Use craft shears to cut out the clear vinyl pattern piece.

2. Transfer the remaining patterns (pages 96–97) onto the paper and cardstock. Use craft shears to cut out the nipple, bottle cap, and milk pieces.

3. Lay the milk pattern piece on a piercing mat and secure it with removable tape. Position the clear vinyl piece over the milk pattern and secure it with removable tape. Position the tracing paper pattern over the clear vinyl piece and secure it with removable tape. Pierce the stitching holes through the tracing paper, the milk pattern piece; and the clear vinyl piece.

4. Remove the tape; then reuse it to attach the milk pattern piece to the vinyl pattern piece from the back side.

5. Use two strands of very light blue embroidery floss to *backstitch* (page 80) the measurement lines on the bottle. This will hold the milk piece in place. Move the removable tape out of your way as you backstitch around the outside edge of the plastic piece.

You don't want to gum up your needle and thread by stitching through the tape, but you do want to use the tape to keep the milk piece in position as you stitch.

6. Adhere the bottle cap piece to the nipple piece with glue stick and then pierce the stitching holes through both layers. Adhere the nipple/cap piece to the clear plastic bottle piece with glue stick.

7. Use two strands of bright pink embroidery floss to *backstitch* on the pattern line on the nipple piece. With two strands of light lavender floss, *backstitch* along the horizontal pattern lines on the cap. Use two strands of very light blue floss to *backstitch* the vertical pattern lines on the cap.

step-by-step directions

Refer to the instructions for piercing holes (page 72).

outside frame card

1. Transfer the patterns (page 96–97) onto the paper and cardstock. Trim the paper and the cardstock on the outside pattern lines using a paper trimmer.

2. Lay the paper and cardstock pieces on the self-healing craft mat and use a craft knife and ruler to cut out the inside pattern lines, creating the window openings. Attach the layers with double-sided tacky tape.

3. Score the center of the card with a bone folder; then fold.

4. Tie a knot in the center of each piece of ribbon. Attach the ribbons to your card by putting a little dab of jewel glue on the back side of each knot.

tip
If you don't have a bone folder, use a butter knife.

customize bébé bottle card

1. Spell out "bébé" or your new baby's name with sweet little baby ID bracelet beads strung onto pearl cotton. Tie the beads on the front side of the frame and add a tight little bow on the opposite side. Secure the knot with a little dot of jewel glue. Don't close the card until the glue is completely dry or it will get glued shut!

2. If you'd like, add a little charm to the beads.

tip
We found it! The lightweight, clear vinyl on a huge roll at the fabric/craft store is perfect to stitch through. The staff was happy to cut off a little strip for us to use for card making.

inside frame card

1. Trim the lime sherbet cardstock to 4" x 6½" (10.2 x 15.2 cm). Apply glue stick around the inside of the lime cardstock, avoiding the outside edges where you will stitch. Adhere the lime cardstock to the lavender cardstock.

2. Pierce holes through both of the layers of cardstock. Following the stitching holes, do all of the *straight stitches* (page 75) slanting left and then do all of the straight stitches slanting right. Look at the photo as you stitch so that you don't get confused about which way the stitches should go.

you'll need
[for picture frame card]

○ tools

transfer tools
ruler
paper trimmer
craft knife
craft shears
paper piercing tools
self-healing craft mat
mouse pad
bone folder
embroidery scissors
chenille needle: size 22
tapestry needle: size 22

○ materials

double-sided tacky tape
four 3" (7.6 cm) ribbons,
    ⅜" (1 cm) wide: bubble
    gum pink
jewel glue
pearl cotton, size 5: bright pink
baby ID bracelet beads
glue stick: extra-strength,
    acid-free
enamel heart charm (optional)

○ papers & cardstocks

paper: dot print
textured cardstock:
    bubble gum pink
cardstock: lavender,
    lime sherbet

key to a happy home

Do you have a friend who has found her perfect match? Are you looking for a creative way to congratulate someone on a new home? We've got the key!

Using only a few basic stitches, you will create this beautiful designer card in an afternoon. A little chain adds some subtle "bling" and saves some stitching time. It's a project that you'll be proud to give—and because you don't need to invest lots of time making it, you won't be tempted to lock it up for yourself.

step-by-step directions

Refer to the instructions for transferring patterns (page 82), scoring (page 66), and piercing holes (page 72).

1. Transfer the patterns (page 98) for the house onto yellow paper; the door, shutters and roof onto violet cardstock; the key onto pewter metallic paper; the tag onto beige cardstock; the tag topper onto pink cardstock. Cut all the patterns out. Use the craft knife to cut out the keyhole and the window in the door.

2. Use craft shears to cut out a 3½" x 3¾" (8.9 x 9.5 cm) rectangle from striped paper. Adhere the house to it with the glue stick. Use the craft knife to cut out the attic window through both layers of paper.

3. Glue the tag topper to the tag. Punch a hole and attach the eyelet.

4. Stamp initials or a greeting on the tag.

5. Pierce all stitching holes following the pattern lines, except for the attic window in the house.

6. With yellow pearl cotton, *backstitch* (page 80) down the sides of the house and *running stitch* (page 76) along the tag topper and along the roof.

7. Using violet pearl cotton, *straight stitch* (page 75) the shutters and *backstitch* around the door.

8. With the brown pearl cotton, *backstitch* around the bottom two windows and flowerbox. Then *stem stitch* (page 81) the small roof and weave through the backstitch on the large roof.

9. *Blanket stitch* (page 79) the grass using green pearl cotton. Alternate yellow, pink, and violet pearl cotton to make *French knot* (page 78) flowers in the flowerbox and along the grass line.

10. Put double-sided tape at the four corners of the underside of the striped paper and adhere it to the front of the blue card. Tape the key at the upper left of the house. Adhere the tag with a foam square.

11. Pierce holes around the key and attic window. *Backstitch* with brown pearl cotton. Connect the key to the tag with a small chain or bit of pearl cotton.

you'll need

tools

transfer tools
ruler
craft shears
craft knife
hole punch
eyelet setter
paper piercing tools
self-healing craft mat
mouse pad
bone folder
embroidery scissors
tapestry needle: size 22
pliers

materials

glue stick: extra-strength, acid-free
eyelet
letter stamps
inkpad: purple
pearl cotton: size 5: yellow, violet, brown, green, pink
double-sided tape
ready-made blank card: blue, silver
tape
adhesive foam squares: double-sided
silver chain

papers & cardstocks

paper: yellow, striped, pewter metallic
cardstock: violet, beige, pink

cactus cocktail

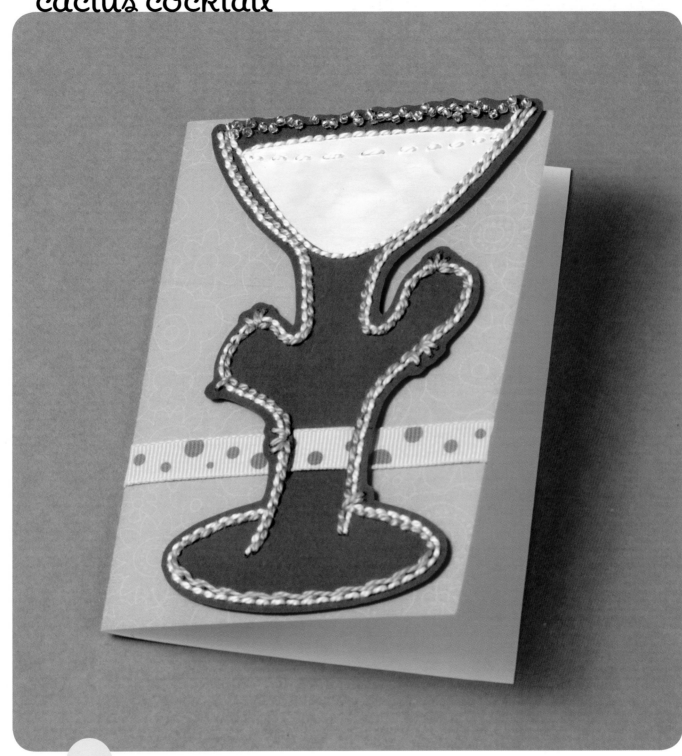

Know someone who needs refreshment? This greeting card is totally cool with its icy rim and fresh cactus design. It makes a perfect cocktail party invite that's sure to impress. Have a blast picking out funky paper to use for the drink! Try endless bead possibilities. This card is so quick and easy to make that you may have to cut yourself off!

step-by-step directions

Refer to the instructions for transferring patterns (page 82), scoring (page 66), and piercing holes (page 72).

1. Transfer the glass pattern (page 99) onto the dark blue cardstock.

2. Transfer the drink pattern (page 99) onto the iridescent paper. Cut it out and glue it into place on the cardstock.

3. Pierce the stitching holes along the pattern lines and randomly around the top rim line of the glass.

4. *Running stitch* (page 76) along the inner rim of the drink pattern with the lemon pearl cotton. *Backstitch* (page 80) along the remainder of the pattern, omitting the top rim of the glass and the cactus needles.

5. Using lime pearl cotton, *backstitch* at the top left, inside the lemon stitching, until you reach the bottom base of the glass. Switch to *stem stitch* (page 81) along the bottom base and then continue to *backstitch* up the remainder of the glass.

6. Complete the cactus with lime pearl cotton *straight stitches* (page 75) for the needles.

7. Thread the beading needle with clear nylon thread. Starting from the back, poke the needle up, thread a clear bead and poke the needle back down through the same hole. Continue until the length of the rim is covered with beads.

8. Cut a slit inside the stitching on both sides of the cactus stem equal to the width of your ribbon. Then slip the ribbon through.

9. Cut the pink floral paper into a 7½" x 5¼" (19.1 x 13.3 cm) rectangle. Using the bone folder, fold it in half to make a 3¾" x 5¼" (9.5 x 13.3 cm) card.

10. Place large pieces of double-sided tape on the back of the cactus and stick it onto the card front. Put a piece of double-sided tape on the bottom ends of the ribbon and wrap around to secure to the card back.

you'll need

tools

ruler
transfer tools
craft scissors
paper piercing tools
self-healing craft mat
mouse pad
bone folder
embroidery scissors
chenille needle: size 22
beading needle

materials

glue stick: extra-strength, acid-free
pearl cotton, size 5: lemon, lime
clear nylon thread
clear beads
4" (10.2 cm) grosgrain ribbon, ⅜" (1 cm) wide: yellow dotted
double-sided tape

papers & cardstocks

paper: iridescent, pink floral print
cardstock: dark blue

lyrical note iPod

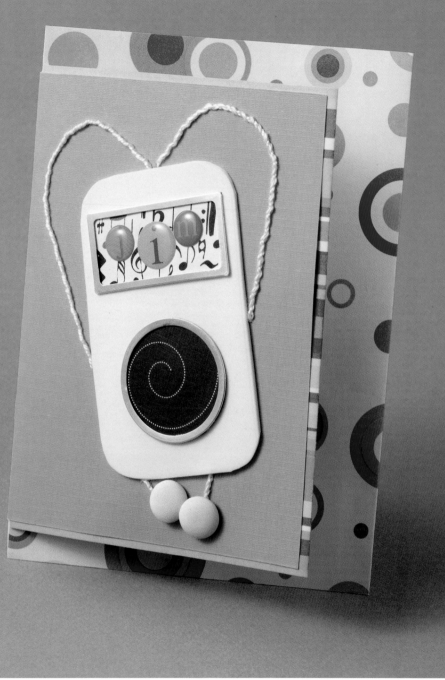

We designed this card for the music and music gizmo fanatics in our lives, our guys.

Make one of these note cards for the music lover in your life. Inside write out those song lyrics that express exactly what you've got on your mind!

step-by-step directions

Refer to the instructions for transferring patterns (page 82), scoring (page 66), and piercing holes (page 72).

1. Transfer all patterns (page 99) onto the craft foam and the card front. Use craft shears to cut out the craft foam shape. Using the paper trimmer, cut the dot paper 9¼" x 6½" (23.6 x 16.5 cm); cut the stripe paper 8½" x 5¾" (21.6 x 14.6 cm); and cut the music print 1" x 2" (2.5 x 5.1 cm). Cut a 1½" (3.8 cm) circle from the swirl paper.

2. Remove the parchment from the inside of the tags. Apply a scant line of jewel glue to the wrong side of the tag rims. Adhere the rectangle tag rim to the music print paper and the circle tag to the swirl print paper. When they are dry, trim away the excess paper from the outside of the tag rims.

3. Apply jewel glue to the wrong side of the tags; then mount them on the craft foam.

4. Pierce the stitching holes in the card.

5. Using white pearl cotton, *backstitch* (page 80) along the stitching lines. Weave white pearl cotton over your backstitches, creating *whipped backstitching* (page 80).

6. Apply jewel glue to the wrong side of the craft foam and buttons; then mount them onto the card.

7. Mark the ~~~~~~~~ ~~~~~~ papers, scor~~~~~ ~~~~~ ~~~~~d.

SPinner
card

inside

you'll need

tools
transfer tools
craft shears
paper trimmer
paper piercing tools
self-healing craft mat
mouse pad
embroidery scissors
tapestry needle: size 22
bone folder

materials
white craft foam (you can
   substitute cardstock or felt)
premade card:
   4¼" x 5½" (10.8 x 14 cm)
parchment tag: rectangle,
   1" x 2" (2.5 x 5.1 cm); circle,
   1½" (3.8 cm) diameter
jewel glue
pearl cotton, size 5 cotton: white
½" (1.3 cm) buttons: white
tape runner adhesive
dome letter stickers

papers & cardstocks
paper: dot, stripe, music print,
   swirl, diameter circle

i wanna iguana

Did you know that iguanas can be affectionate, litter-box trainable, and even walked on a leash? Although they're not necessarily known for it, these cold-blooded creatures have warm hearts and make great companions.

This design is easy to create. You'll have fun picking out paper for his tropical environment and the transparency adds a unique camouflage element that'll leave friends asking, "How'd you do that?"

step-by-step directions

Refer to the instructions for transferring patterns (page 82), scoring (page 66), and piercing holes (page 72).

1. Transfer the iguana body pattern (page 102) onto yellow paper and transfer the shadow pattern onto blue transparency paper. Then transfer the eye onto white cardstock, making the pupil with a black pen.

2. Cut out all the pieces and use one small piece of double-sided tape at the center of each to adhere the three together.

3. Pierce the stitching holes down the iguana's back. *Straight stitch* (page 75) with pink pearl cotton. Then add a *French knot* (page 78) with blue pearl cotton at the top of each stitch.

4. Transfer the card pattern onto flower paper. Use the bone folder to score; fold in half to make a 4" x 4" (10.2 x 10.2 cm) card with a 3/8" (1 cm) gap at the bottom.

5. Cut a 4" x 1" (10.2 x 2.5 cm piece rectangle from the blue transparency paper. Run a line of double-sided tape across the top and adhere it to the inside of the card, so that 3/8" (1 cm) sticks over the edge and aligns with the card back.

6. Place the iguana at the top right of the card, so that his back hangs over the edge, and stick him down with one piece of double-sided tape. Then, put a mouse pad under the open card and pierce the rest of the stitching holes.

7. Using pink pearl cotton, *backstitch* (page 80), around the iguana body and mouth. Also *straight stitch* through every other hole at the bottom of the card.

8. Using yellow pearl cotton, *backstitch* the tongue and around the eye. Then make a *French knot* for the nostril and *straight stitch* through every other hole at the bottom of the card.

9. Thread the needle with blue pearl cotton and make alternating *French knots* at the top and bottom of every straight stitch at the bottom of the card.

10. Finally, cut a small piece of blue pearl cotton and tie a small bow. Put a dab of glue on the tip of both tails so they don't fray and put a dab on the back of the bow. Stick the bow in with the bottom row of French knots.

you'll need

tools

transfer tools
ruler
pencil
black pen
craft shears
1/8" (3 mm) paper punch
paper piercing tools
self-healing craft mat
mouse pad
bone folder
embroidery scissors
tapestry needle: size 22

materials

double-sided tape
jewel glue
pearl cotton, size 5:
   pink, blue, yellow

papers & cardstocks

paper: flower print,
   yellow paper
transparent paper: blue
cardstock: white

ribbonbird peek-a-boo card

Rare Ribbonbirds are amusing additions to card maker's creations. Let your own species evolve when you substitute ribbons printed with dots, swirls, or stripes. Add beads or crystals for fanciful tail feathers. The Ribbonbird can adapt to a variety of habitats—glue him onto any surface that won't get wet (i.e.: won't need to be washed). Something like a storage container or notebook would be ideal, as the Ribbonbird isn't a water fowl!

style option:

The ambience on the front of this card leads you to believe that you know what to expect when you open it, but it's only a hint of the whimsical surprise inside. For different occasions, put the card together first (without the tree limb and leaf circles, of course); then position a photo or part of a printed paper inside the card so that only a hint of your surprise is revealed in the "peek-a-boo" circle.

you'll need
[for peek-a-boo card]

◯ tools

transfer tools
paper trimmer
craft shears
ruler
craft knife
fabric shears
paper piercing tools
self-healing craft mat
mouse pad
embroidery scissors
tapestry needle: size 22
crewel embroidery needle:
    medium

◯ materials

glue stick: extra-strength,
    acid-free
pearl cotton, size 5: brown
3" (7.6 cm) grosgrain ribbons,
    ½" (1.3 cm) wide: light
    green, medium green,
    dark green
3" (7.6 cm) grosgrain ribbons,
    ¼" (6 mm) wide: light
    green, medium green,
    dark green, brown
fabric glue
9" (22.9 cm) grosgrain ribbon,
    ½" (1.3 cm) wide: brown
cotton embroidery floss: green
embellishment tag
adhesive square

◯ papers & cardstocks

paper: tropical foliage,
    orange print
cardstock: kiwi striped print
textured cardstock: bright blue

step-by-step directions

Refer to the instructions for transferring patterns (page 82), scoring (page 66), and piercing holes (page 72).

peek-a-boo card

1. Transfer the patterns (page 100–101) onto the paper and cardstock. Cut out the paper shapes with craft shears. Cut the bright blue cardstock to 4½" x 6" (11.4 x 15.2 cm) and the tropical foliage paper to 5½" x 7" (14 x 17.8 cm) using the paper trimmer.

2. Mark the center of the kiwi striped cardstock, score it with the bone folder, and then fold the crease.

3. Apply glue stick to the wrong side of the orange print paper shape and attach it to the front of the card. Apply glue stick to the wrong side of the tropical print paper shape and attach it to the front of the card. Open the card. Pierce the stitching holes through all three layers and use a craft knife to cut out the "peek-a-boo" hole.

4. *Running stitch* (page 76) along the stitching lines with brown pearl cotton. Weave over the running stitches around the "peek-a-boo" hole, creating *whipped running stitches* (page 77).

5. Trim the ends of the green ribbons at angles with fabric shears. Tie the green ribbons together in the center with the narrow brown ribbon. Attach the ribbon bundle with fabric glue.

6. Apply glue stick to the wrong side of the tropical print rectangle and attach it to the inside of the card. Apply glue stick to the wrong side of the blue cardstock and attach it to the tropical print paper. Spread fabric glue onto the wide brown ribbon "tree trunk" and adhere it to the card. Apply glue stick to the wrong side of the tropical print circles and attach them to the card.

7. Pierce the stitching holes through all three layers.

8. *Straight stitch* (page 75) in one direction and then the other, creating *cross-stitches* (page 75) with brown pearl cotton. *Straight stitch* in one direction and then the other, creating *zigzag stitches* (page 75) with two strands of green embroidery floss.

9. Tie a 3" (7.6 cm) length of brown pearl cotton to the tag.

10. Apply an adhesive square to the wrong side of the ribbonbird on the wing right behind the eye. Apply a few drops of fabric glue to the wrong side of the ribbons where they attach to the bird's body. Peel away the backing on the adhesive square. Apply a drop of fabric glue to the wrong side of the yellow beak shape. Position the bird onto the card.

11. Adhere the tag to the card; then slip the pearl cotton under the tip of the bird's beak.

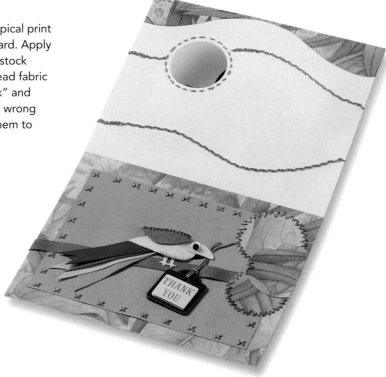

the elusive ribbonbird

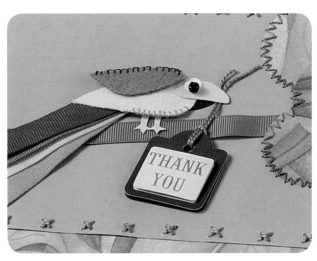

1. Transfer the patterns (page 100) onto the felt and cardstock. Use craft shears to cut out the cardstock beak and feet pieces.

2. Mark the stitching dots on the wing and body with a water-erasable marker. With fabric shears, cut out the felt shapes.

3. Punch out a ¼" (6 mm) dot from the white cardstock. Pierce a single hole through it. Sew on the black bead using one strand of black embroidery floss. Secure the thread tails to the back of the dot with tape. Trim away any excess tape from around the edges of the dot. Adhere the dot to the yellow beak piece with a small drop of fabric glue.

4. *Blanket stitch* (page 79) along the stitch markings on the body with one strand of orange embroidery floss and along the stitch markings on the wing with dark blue.

5. Spread fabric glue onto the wrong side of the wing and adhere it to the body. Attach the yellow beak to the right side of the body, the black beak piece to the wrong side of the body, and the feet to the wrong side of the body with fabric glue.

6. Arrange the tail feather ribbons; then glue them together with fabric glue. Attach the assembled tail feathers to the wrong side of the body with fabric glue.

you'll need
[for ribbonbird]

○ **tools**

transfer tools
craft shears
fabric shears
paper piercing tools
self-healing craft mat
mouse pad
embroidery scissors
crewel embroidery needle:
    medium
¼" (6 mm) hole punch

○ **materials**

water-erasable fabric marker
felt: light green, bright green,
    2" x 1" (5.1 x 2.5 cm) each
black bead
cotton embroidery floss:
    black, orange, dark blue
removable tape
fabric glue
3" (7.6 cm) grosgrain ribbons:
    ½" (1.3 cm) wide: red,
    orange, yellow, blue

○ **cardstocks**

cardstock: yellow, black, white

tip

To make it easier to cut out tiny pieces, first cut out the pattern pieces; then lay the cut-out pattern pieces on the cardstock. Lightly attach the pattern pieces to the cardstock with removable tape. Now cut out the shapes—ahhh—so much more manageable than trying to handle itsy-bitsy pieces while cutting. When you're finished cutting, carefully peel away the tape.

cheeky monkey

In a pinch? Keep this funky monkey on hand so it never happens again. He's perfect for grownups or kids and all occasions. We used a general "word" paper, but you can choose any paper to match your theme. You can even write on plain paper to create your own: try different font styles, colors, and even include the recipient's name. When you're the designer, you'll never have to search for an ideal card again!

step-by-step directions

Refer to the instructions for transferring patterns (page 82), scoring (page 66), and piercing holes (page 72).

1. Transfer the patterns (page 103) for the head and ears onto brown cardstock, the eyes onto white cardstock, and the face onto tan cardstock. Cut them out.

2. Assemble the whole monkey head onto a piece of violet cardstock with glue stick. Next, pierce the stitching holes along the pattern lines.

3. *Backstitch* (page 80) with brown pearl cotton around the head, eyes, face, and mouth. Make two *French knots* (page 78) for the nostrils.

4. *Blanket stitch* (page 79) the ears (or do a *backstitch* followed by *straight stitches* [page 75] for a slightly cleaner look), using violet pearl cotton.

5. Transfer the small circle pattern onto the word paper. Then cut it out and use double-sided tape to adhere the monkey face to the middle.

6. Fold a piece of violet cardstock in half, align the large circle outline pattern, and transfer it onto the cardstock (the dotted line across the top of the pattern signifies the fold of the card).

7. Glue the small circle with the monkey onto the larger circle card. Pierce the stitching holes around the inner circle.

8. Finish with *French knots* around the inner circle, using the coral pearl cotton.

you'll need

tools

transfer tools
craft shears
paper piercing tools
self-healing craft mat
mouse pad
bone folder
embroidery scissors
tapestry needle: size 22

materials

glue stick: extra-strength, acid-free
pearl cotton, size 5: brown, violet, coral
double-sided tape

papers & cardstocks

paper: word print
cardstock: brown, tan, white, violet

tip

Take just a few extra moments to give your cards a professional finish. Cover the back of your stitches with a piece of paper or cardstock, attaching it with double-sided tacky tape.

gift package & two-fold card

When you find yourself in need of inspiration or you'd like to see how other crafters are doing things, take a class. Even if you're a pro, there's always some new technique or material that you can pick up on when you're working in a group.

We enjoy taking classes at the Stamp & Scrap Art store in Champaign, Illinois, where a delightful teacher, Dianne Smith, shares her innovative methods for creating a host of cards. She suggests using stencils, rubber stamps, and cookie cutters as handy sources for images to stitch up on cards.

In Dianne's "stitched cards" class we traced this gift package stencil, pierced the stitching holes, and stitched the outline onto a small gift enclosure style card.

Back in our studio, we devised this colorful paper appliqué technique twist that enhances the already charming design.

step-by-step directions

Refer to the instructions for transferring patterns (page 82), scoring (page 66), and piercing holes (page 72).

gift package appliqué

1. Transfer the patterns (pages 104–106) onto the cardstock and paper. Trim the light blue cardstock to size with the paper trimmer.

2. Position the stencil on the light blue cardstock securing it with removable tape. Trace the stencil shapes onto the cardstock using a pencil. Remove the tape.

3. Repeat step 2 on the pink cardstock. Use craft scissors to cut out the pink ribbon shapes.

4. Repeat step 2 on the flowered print paper. Use craft scissors to cut out the gift box shapes.

5. Spread glue stick on the wrong side of the ribbon shapes and adhere them to the blue cardstock. Spread glue stick on the wrong side of the gift box shapes and adhere them to the blue cardstock.

6. Pierce stitching holes along all the outlines.

7. Use two strands of pink embroidery floss to *backstitch* (page 80) along the ribbon outlines and two strands of peach embroidery floss to *running stitch* (page 76) along the package outline.

8. Cut out a peach flower from the flowered print paper. Punch a center hole and attach a mini brad to the flower center. Adhere the flower to the card with a glue dot.

9. Now it's time to decide! You can be almost finished and make this into a cute tag by punching a hole at the top center and tying a ribbon through it or you could take a little more time to make it into a darling tag/card (see page 61) or you can go the distance and mount it onto a two-fold card (page 62) for a spectacular presentation!

you'll need

[for gift package appliqué]

tools

transfer tools
pencil
paper trimmer
craft scissors
paper piercing tools
self-healing craft mat
mouse pad
embroidery scissors
crewel embroidery needle, fine
hole punch
brass gift package stencil

materials

removable tape
glue stick: extra-strength, acid-free
cotton embroidery floss: pink, peach
mini brads
glue dots

papers & cardstocks

paper: flowered print
cardstock: pink, light blue

tip
See page 65 for information on protecting and posting delicate cards.

stitched name and label holder

1. Transfer the label pattern (page 106) onto the blue cardstock and use craft scissors to cut it out.

2. Lightly scuff the edges of the cardstock with sandpaper until you have the effect you'd like. Punch holes for the brads.

3. Transfer the pattern for your chosen name or word onto the dark butter cardstock. (See page 84 for how to work with the alphabets provided, or freehand your own lettering with a pencil.)

4. Pierce the stitching pattern. Erase the pencil marks. *Backstitch* (page 80) the lettering with two strands of pink floss. Tape the beginning and ending tails to the wrong side of the cardstock.

5. Lay the label holder facedown and spread a thin line of jewel glue along the edges. Turn the label holder over and position it over the lettering. Let the glue dry; then trim away the excess dark butter cardstock from the outside of the label holder.

6. Punch holes for the brads through the dark butter cardstock. Insert the brads.

you'll need

[for name and label hol•

○ **tools**

transfer tools
pencil
eraser
craft scissors
⅛" (3 mm) hole punch
paper piercing tools
self-healing craft mat
mouse pad
embroidery scissors
crewel embroidery needle: fir•

○ **materials**

sandpaper
cotton embroidery floss: pink
tape
jewel glue
mini brads: bubble blue

○ **papers & cardstocks**

paper: flowered print/peach
    solid, 2" (5.1 cm) square
cardstock: light blue,
    dark butter

tip
An emery board is a good substitute for sandpaper.

step-by-step directions

cutout flower tag

1. Cut out five or more flowers from the flowered print paper. Punch holes in the centers for the brads. Attach the brads to each center. Adhere the cutout flowers to the vellum tag with mini glue dots.

2. Fold the gingham ribbon in half. Lay the folded ribbon on the vellum tag. Lay the vellum tag on the craft mat. Use the point of a craft knife to cut a small hole for the brad. Attach the brad.

you'll need
[for flower tag]

tools

craft scissors
craft knife
⅛" (3 mm) hole punch
self-healing craft mat

materials

mini brads: bubble blue,
    tangerine, rosy, white
metal-rimmed vellum circle tag
mini glue dots
3½" (8.9 cm) gingham
    ribbon, ¼" (6 mm) wide:
    blue and white

papers

paper: flowered print/peach
    solid

two-fold card

card front

1. Transfer the patterns (page 105) onto the paper and cardstock. Use the paper trimmer to cut the straight pattern lines. Score and crease the fold lines with a bone folder.

2. Use the glue stick to attach the peach paper (the reverse side of the flower print paper) to the cardstock. Use the glue stick to mount the blue cardstock (with your stitched design) onto the peach paper.

3. Adhere 6" (15.2 cm) of tangerine ribbon across the top front of the card with a strip of double-sided tape. Fold the tails around to the back and inside of the card.

4. Refer to the photo and pierce the stitching holes. You'll be piercing holes through the right side of the ribbon.

5. Refer to the photo and *running stitch* (page 76) only where you see stitches on the picture, using the tangerine pearl cotton and a chenille needle.

6. Adhere the label holder to the ribbon with glue dots.

7. Poke a hole for the rosy brad on the right side of the ribbon using a craft knife and craft mat. Attach the brad.

tip Add photos to this two-fold card to turn it into a sweet mini album.

inside

1. Cut the blue dot paper 5¼" x 4⅛" (13.3 x 10.5 cm). Score and crease it. Mount it to the inside of the card with tape runner adhesive.

2. Mount the strips of flowered print paper and peach paper to the inside of the card with tape runner adhesive.

3. Adhere 7" (17.8 cm) of tangerine ribbon from the top to bottom, covering the join of the blue dot and peach papers, with a strip of double-sided tape. Fold the tails around to the back side of the card.

back of card

1. Cover the back of the card with leftover pieces of flower print paper to cover up the peach ribbon tail.

2. Wrap 12" (30.5 cm) of blue ribbon along the edge of the card with a strip of double-sided tape. Begin 1" (2.5 cm) from the top in the inside, take the ribbon around to and up the outside, and fold the tail over the top back into the inside of the card.

3. Use double-sided tape to attach the cutout flower tag to the blue ribbon.

4. Cut 8" (20.3 cm) of tangerine ribbon. Tie the ribbon into a tight little bow. Trim the ends at angles. Adhere the bow to the wrong side of the vellum tag with jewel glue. Allow the glue to dry completely before you close the card. You wouldn't want a bit of glue to stick your card shut and then tear the paper when it's opened!

you'll need
[for two-fold card]

tools

transfer tools
paper trimmer
craft knife
paper piercing tools
self-healing craft mat
mouse pad
bone folder
embroidery scissors
chenille needle: size 22

materials

glue stick: extra-strength, acid-free
21" (35.6 cm) grosgrain ribbon, ⅜" (1 cm) wide: tangerine
double-sided tape
12" (30.5 cm) grosgrain ribbon, ⅜" (1 cm) wide: blue
pearl cotton, size 5: tangerine
glue dots
mini brad: rosy
tape runner adhesive
vellum tag
jewel glue

papers & cardstocks

papers: flowered print/peach solid, blue dot print
cardstock: dark butter

easy envelopes

A gorgeous handmade card deserves to be received in impeccable condition. By far, the very best way to give a custom-made card is to personally hand deliver it. That way you know the card will arrive in perfect shape and you'll be able to see the delighted expression and enjoy the admiring responses from the lucky recipient!

When you can't hand deliver your card and you've got to post it, take these precautions to ensure that your card has a safe journey:

Simple, flat cards will travel just fine in a cardstock envelope, but handmade envelopes with stitching on them could run into problems going through machines at the post office. To avoid a nasty accident, slip your beautiful envelope inside a regular envelope (a cardboard mailer is even better). Address and attach postage to the outside envelope.

When mailing any handmade card, it can't hurt to label it "Please Hand Stamp" and "FRAGILE."

Make sure that you attach enough postage. Odd sizes and shapes, like squares, require extra postage. The best way to be sure that you have the correct postage is to bring your package to the post office to have them advise you on the right amount.

Cards that have beads, buttons, or other embellishments on them need to be sent in a "bubble envelope" for a bit more protection. Bubble envelopes are squishy and bend easily, so add the needed stability by positioning the back of your card onto a piece of cardboard that's been cut slightly smaller than the bubble envelope.

step-by-step directions

Refer to the instructions for transferring patterns (page 82), scoring (page 66), and piercing holes (page 72).

1. Create a pattern to fit your card! Refer to the diagrams on pages 107–108 and draw a rectangle following these dimensions:

   BODY: ½" (1.3 cm) wider than the width of the card and ¼" (6 mm) taller than its height.

   BOTTOM FLAP: ½" (1.3 cm) wider than the width of the card and ½" (1.3 cm) shorter than its height.

   TOP FLAP: 1½" (3.8 cm) high for cards under 4" (10.2 cm) tall;
   2" (5.1 cm) high for cards over 4" (10.2 cm) high.

2. Cut out along the outside lines with a paper trimmer. Score the fold lines with a bone folder. Fold the bottom flap up.
   Pierce stitching holes through the bottom flap and body. Stitch the bottom flap and body together using any stitch. Fold the top flap down.

you'll need

[for custom envelope]

○ tools

> ruler
> pencil
> paper trimmer
> paper piercing tools
> self-healing craft mat
> mouse pad
> bone folder
> embroidery scissors
> chenille needle

○ materials

> pearl cotton or floss

○ papers & cardstocks

> to suit the card

card boxes

Fragile and delicate cards, like those with cutout flowers or dimensional effects, require sturdy containers. Wrap your card in bubble wrap and place it in a sturdy little gift box. Craft stores have plain boxes and some that are covered with decorative paper. If you're a perfectionist, you'll probably want to decorate the box to match your card. Hand-deliver or slip your bundle into a bubble envelope and it's good to go.

tools and materials

CUTTING, PUNCHING, PIERCING

Shears have a small handle for your thumb and a larger handle for your other fingers. Scissors have same-sized handles.

craft scissors and shears

They're for cutting paper, cardstock, and other things that you shouldn't cut with your embroidery scissors or fabric shears.

embroidery scissors and fabric shears

With small blades and very sharp, tiny, pointed tips, embroidery scissors are used for trimming threads and snipping out bad stitches. Never use them for anything else. Keep them in a sheath or case to protect them and yourself!

Use fabric shears for cutting only fabric and threads; they will become dull if they are used to cut paper.

decorative-edged craft scissors and shears

These come in tons of styles; we find that we use a scallop and zigzag more than any others. Pinking shears have a zigzag edge, but they're a lot more expensive than craft scissors/shears because they're made to cut fabric.

Some decorative-edged scissors/shears have very short blades, making them difficult to use because after cutting only a short way you have to stop and try to match the cutting pattern before the next cut. Try to buy decorative-edged craft scissors/shears that have longer blades.

tip

For crisp, clean professional looking folds, score the paper first. Place a ruler along the fold line and drag the tip of a bone folder down the fold line. After folding, use the broad side of the bone folder to press and smooth the crease

Craft scissors (1), craft shears (2), embroidery scissors (3), fabric shears (4), decorative-edged scissors (5), decorative-edged shears (6).

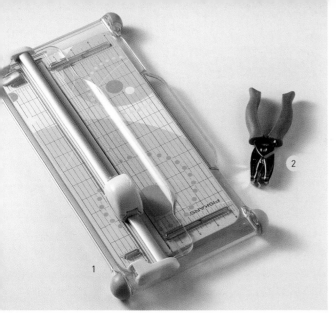

Paper trimmer (1) and hole punch (2).

hole punches

Hole punches come in the shape of circles, hearts, stars, flowers, and endless other choices.

Start your collection with round ¼" (6 mm) and ⅛" (3 mm) hole punches. You'll need them to make the holes at the top of tags. They're handy for making holes for brads and eyelets as well.

paper trimmer

This is a huge time-saver for making perfect straight cuts.

craft knife

The unbelievably sharp, pointy blade can make those tiny little cuts a breeze. Be extremely careful with this tool.

paper piercers

To pierce holes in your paper or cardstock, you can use a paper piercer, awl, stiletto, a large needle, or a florist's pin. There are times when you'll be stitching with a thick thread-like pearl cotton and will need bigger stitching holes. Other times, when you're doing fine delicate stitching with just a strand or two of embroidery floss, you'll need smaller stitching holes. Before you pierce the holes for your project, consider which paper piercing tool will make the hole size that will work best with your needle and thread. You might even want to pierce a few holes on a scrap of your stitching surface and test a few stitches to make sure that everything will work out well.

self-healing craft mat

Believe us, we know this firsthand—a self-healing craft mat is an absolute necessity whenever you're using a craft knife or piercing holes. It will save the surface of your worktable from irreparable damage.

mouse pad

Yep, the same little guy that you use with your computer mouse. Lay it on top of your self-healing craft mat to safely pierce holes.

see-through metal edged ruler

You have to use a metal edge for cutting with a craft knife. A craft knife is so sharp that it will whittle away at a plastic ruler and give you wavy or ragged cut lines. A see-through ruler is so unbelievably handy that you won't know how you ever got along without one. You can line up and trim quickly because you can see right where everything is. Brilliant!

double sided tape runner

This tape dispenser is an essential tool for card makers.

Paper piercer (1), mouse pad (2), self-healing cutting mat (3), double-sided tape runner (4), see-through ruler (5), craft knife (6).

NEEDLES

The right needle makes embroidering delightful; the wrong needle makes it harder than it has to be. A needle's job is to make a hole in the stitching surface so that the thread can pass through easily. If the needle is too narrow, the thread will fray and break. If the needle is too wide, you can have trouble getting it through your paper, it might leave holes, and your stitches will look sloppy.

The size of the needle depends on the size of the thread. The correct size needle should be slightly wider at the eye (the hole for the thread) than the thickness of your thread. For help selecting a needle size, check the materials list with each project or the chart below.

Store needles in a pincushion, wool/felt needle book, or wooden tube needle case to keep them sharp, clean, dry, and free from corrosion.

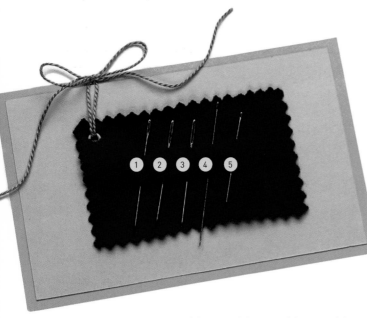

NEEDLES: crewel or embroidery (1), chenille (2), tapestry (3), beading (4), sharps (5).

crewel or embroidery needles

These have a sharp point for piercing fabric. They have an elongated oval eye that makes it easy to thread stranded embroidery floss. Some companies use the name "crewel" on their packaging for embroidery needles.

chenille needles

These also have a sharp point that will pierce through fabric and other threads, but they are thicker and longer and have a longer, bigger eye than crewel needles. The large eye allows you to thread pearl cotton, yarn, thick threads, or stranded embroidery floss.

tapestry needles

Tapestry needles are similar to chenille needles, except they have a blunt tip. They are used for stitches worked in the surface threads, such as the whipping on running and backstitches or the weaving on woven and double-woven backstitches. Tapestry needles are used most for stitching on paper and cardstock.

beading needles

Longer and thinner than ordinary sewing needles, beading needles are about the same diameter their whole length, with a tiny round eye that beads can easily pass over.

sharps

These are general sewing needles. They have small round eyes and sharp points.

Crewel or Embroidery Needle Size	Floss Strands
10	one strand of six-stranded
8	three strands of six-stranded
3	six strands of six-stranded
6	#5 pearl cotton

Tapestry or Chenille Needle Size	Floss Strands
26	one or two strand of six-stranded
27	three or four strands of six-stranded
22	six strands of six-stranded
22	#5 pearl cotton

ADHESIVES

If you're planning to make keepsake cards that will be in good condition years from now, it's important to use archival-quality acid-free products. It is especially important to use acid-free adhesives because adhesives that aren't acid-free will discolor, stain, and ruin your work over time.

tape

Use standard, adhesive on one side, tape to secure thread tails to cardstock.

removable tape

Removable tape is not as sticky as standard tape. It won't tear paper when it's removed. Use removable tape to hold patterns in place for transferring and cutting.

glue stick

Glue stick adhesive dries into a hard, non-sticky bond. It's the best choice for attaching surfaces that will be stitched later. It's not a good choice for mounting paper/cardstock permanently.

jewel glue

This glue works especially well for adhering odd-shaped embellishments that don't lie flat. Jewel glue dries perfectly clear. It does require some drying time.

fabric glue

Fabric glue works best for gluing fabrics and threads together. Once dry, it's washable and flexible. Fabric glue is the only choice for gluing an appliqué onto clothing.

double-sided tape runner

A tape runner is a basic papercrafting tool. It's a great time-saver; just guide the tape runner wherever you want an instant bond. Once pressed down, it's permanent.

double-sided adhesive foam

Double-sided adhesive foam comes in a variety of shapes, sizes, and thicknesses. They add a strong 3-D bond.

double-sided tacky tape

This tape is super sticky. It permanently tacks down things that might not stay stuck with other adhesives. It's perfect for keeping ribbon in place.

glue dots

Glue dots come in different sizes and thicknesses. They're great for adhering small, flat embellishments like buttons, brads, or craft flowers. The have zero drying time and a strong bond.

tip

The world can be a messy place. Wash your hands before you start to work on a project; then keep food and drinks far away from them. Carry a few individually packaged wet-wipes in your project kit and you'll be ready to make a clean start when you're on the go. When you're not working on your project, store it in a resealable plastic bag to keep it clean and dry.

Keep *all* your supplies in a portable storage container so you'll have everything ready whenever and wherever you get the itch to stitch!

Pearl cotton (1), cotton floss (2), linen floss (3), rayon floss (4), variegated floss (5), metallic and pearlescent threads (6).

tip

SAFETY WARNING: Always keep sewing and craft supplies out of the reach of babies, small children and those who may improperly handle them.

Choosing and working with threads is a pure pleasure. They come in every color imaginable and offer sheen and sparkle, too!

pearl cotton thread

Pearl cotton thread is the quintessential thread for beginners. Everybody loves the lustrous sheen and vast color selection. It comes in three weights, #3, #5, and #8—the highest number being the lightest weight—and is tightly twisted so you use it as one thread. You can't, and shouldn't try, to separate strands.

six-strand embroidery floss

Floss is available in numerous fibers: cotton, linen, and rayon, to name a few. It comes in almost every color you can imagine, even variegated and sumptuous hand-dyed colors. When you separate floss into individual strands and recombine them, you can achieve a variety of effects depending on the number of strands used. One strand produces very fine lines and delicate details. All six strands can be used to create thick, bold stitches.

metallic thread, specialty threads, and other fun fibers

These are the icing on the cake! When you feel confident about your skill with pearl cotton thread and embroidery floss, you're ready to move on to metallic and specialty threads. They're not recommended for rookies because they tend to fray, untwist, tangle, or snag after a while. The first line of defense is to use shorter lengths of thread. Use a slightly larger needle than you would normally, so it makes a hole big enough to not "rough up" the thread. As soon as you notice a thread looking thinner, frayed, or worn, stop using it and begin again with a fresh thread. Despite their trickiness, don't hesitate to embroider with these sweet threads. The more you stitch with them, the more you'll love using them. Also try using a thread conditioner to keep things moving along smoothly.

thread storage

Before you know it, you'll have lots of threads and flosses. What's the best way to keep everything organized so you can find what you want for your next project? We keep each color of floss or thread in an individual, snack-size, resealable plastic bag. Write the color number on the outside of the bag with a permanent marker. We like to save the label with the color number and brand information in the bag as well. The plastic bags keep your threads clean, dry, and fuzz-free and will keep small humans and pet friends safe. When you've amassed a collection of little plastic bags of thread, organize them by color into a small storage box. Plastic shoe boxes with snap-on lids or photo storage boxes work well for this. Label each box with the colors that it contains. Storage units with shallow drawers are handy for storing thread, too.

Sponge (1), needle threaders (2), needle puller (3), thimbles (4), thread conditioner (5).

These little notions can make a big difference. They can make your stitches look great and make crafting easier, too.

sponge

Some stitchers like to use a small sponge to moisten threads before threading into a needle and to straighten threads. The sponge must be perfectly clean and should be dedicated to this use only.

needle threaders

Have trouble threading a needle? Try this fine wire loop that passes through the eye of the needle easily. You just insert the thread into the wire loop and slowly pull the needle threader back through the eye of the needle.

needle puller

A small rubber disc helps you "get a grip" on your needle when you're having trouble pulling the needle through some thick cardstock.

thimbles and needle pushers

These protect the middle finger of your stitching hand—or the finger you use to push the needle—while you're embroidering. Our favorite thimble is a leather quilting thimble with a small metal disk at the fingertip. It's open at the top for your nail tip to stick out. The indentations on the surface of a steel thimble hold the needle in place while you push it through the fabric. You might start out without a thimble, but when your finger gets sore, you'll be happy you've got one on hand (so to speak).

thread conditioner

This product helps prevent fraying and tangling. It's especially helpful when using metallic and specialty threads. You simply draw the thread across the conditioner and then smooth it with your fingers. We use Thread Heaven.

Before You Stitch: Prepare!

Stitching techniques traditionally used for fabric can also be used for papercrafting. You can attach vellum and embellishments with stitches, make a pocket to hold a note, or stitch borders, titles, and designs.

You can embroider letters and words by drawing them freehand or by tracing letter templates, stencils, or the alphabet patterns in the back of this book. Use a pencil to draw on paper or cardstock and use disappearing marker on fabric.

For a finished look, fill the letters in with colored pencil, chalk, slitter, beads or paint before stitching. Or try a new technique, fabric or paper appliqué (used with the Gift Package on page 68).

The secret for successful stitching on paper and cardstock: pierce holes for the stitches.

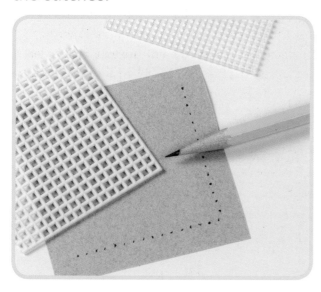

1. Use a pencil to mark the paper/cardstock with dots where you want the stitches. Most of the patterns have dots on them for you to use as a guide for piercing holes. When you want to create your own designs, just use a regular pencil to mark the paper/cardstock with dots where you want the stitches. For evenly spaced marks we use plastic needlepoint mesh. It comes in different sizes, so you can choose a mesh that has the spacing you prefer. For whimsical, homemade-looking stitches, just poke holes randomly as you go along the pattern outline.

2. Place a self-healing mat on your work surface. On top of that, put your mouse pad, facedown.

3. Lay the cardstock on the mouse pad and use a paper piercer, such as an awl, stiletto, large chenille needle, or florist's pin to pierce holes where you've marked stitching holes.

4. Erase the pencil marks.

5. Use a tapestry needle to lace your thread through the holes with a straight up-and-down stabbing motion.

6. Secure the beginning and ending thread tails on the back of the paper with tape rather than knots.

tip

Use a florist's pin to pierce tiny holes for little stitches made of a strand or two of embroidery floss, stitches that are spaced close together, or stitches that are close to the edge of your stitching surface. Tiny holes are less likely to perforate your paper/cardstock.

Use a bigger piercing tool like an awl or stiletto to pierce larger holes for pearl cotton stitches and large stitches.

When you open a new skein of thread or embroidery floss:

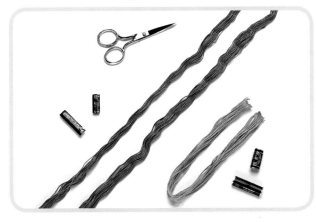

1. Remove the labels and save the label that has the color number on it.

2. Untwist the pearl thread. Lay out the pearl thread or floss into an oval shape.

3. Cut through the pearl thread strands at both ends of the oval, so you have two bundles of 12" (30.5 cm) pieces. Cut through the floss at only one end of the oval, so you have one bundle of 12" (30.5 cm) pieces.

FLOSS POINTERS

Often you need to separate one, two, or more strands of floss from a six-strand length. To keep them from tangling, remove just one strand of floss at a time. After cutting the floss into 12" (30.5 cm) pieces, hold the top of one piece in your hand. Use the other hand to separate one end from the group. Pull that strand straight up and out from the rest. The remaining strands will probably bunch up as you remove it, but you can easily smooth them back in place. Repeat the process to remove each individual strand that you need.

Floss should be straightened before stitching to produce smooth, even stitches. Straightening is also an effective way to revive threads that are creased from being tightly wound on a cardboard or plastic bobbin or for threads that have been crumpled up.

Slightly moisten each individual strand with a drop of water; use the tips of your fingers (or a small, damp sponge) to smooth out and spread the moisture along the length of the strand. The strand should be barely moist, not wet, and should dry completely before you thread your needle.

You can blend strands to create customized colors and special effects. First, straighten each individual strand. Then lay out the straightened strands with the ends aligned and smooth them out along their length. Don't twist the strands. Skim the group as one combined strand across the surface of a thread conditioner. Thread your needle and trim both ends even. Tape the tail of your thread to the back of your paper/cardstock, then start stitching.

thread the needle

Through the ages, millions of needles have been threaded by people who put the end of the thread into their mouths to wet the tip. Some discerning needleworkers use a small sponge and water for moistening thread. Either way will work. Once the tip of the thread is moistened, use your embroidery scissors to snip the tip, either at an angle or straight across. Pinch the tip, aim, and thread it through the needle eye.

Having a little trouble? Try threading the needle from its other side. Occasionally, a needle eye is smaller on one side than the other. Still no luck? Don't get frustrated. Try using a time-saving and very inexpensive needle threader (page 71).

tip

Every project is a little different. The piercing holes are considered part of the pattern, but some projects work better if you wait to pierce the holes until you've already done some assembly. Make sure to read through the project instructions before you start crafting just to make sure you don't pierce prematurely.

Stitching on Paper and Cardstock

The running stitch and cross-stitch are favorites of paper crafters, but you can do so many more! Play with a variety of embroidery stitches on paper or cardstock before using them on a project. Satin stitch, however, doesn't work well on paper because the stitches are so close together that the paper tends to tear. You can embroider satin stitches on fabric and then attach it to your cardstock with double-sided tape.

tip

Here are instructions for all the stitches used in the projects of Greeting Cards in Stitches plus a few extras that have gorgeous special effects. The examples are hand stitched on cardstock and paper and are shown at their actual size. All the stitches can be done on paper and cardstock (or fabric). In these instructions, we're going to call whatever you're stitching on—whether paper, cardstock, or fabric—the "surface."

- Start all of your stitches on the wrong side of your stitching surface.
- Use a straight up-and-down stabbing motion, pulling the thread all the way through to zthe front or back of your stitching surface with each motion. It will help you to keep your stitches even.
- Keep your stitches flat against your stitching surface; avoid loopy and loose as well as tight, surface-scrunching tension.
- Put the "how to" illustration of the stitch you're learning where you can see it and refer to it as you take each step.
- Before starting a project, try stitches that are new to you on a paper scrap until you're happy about the way they look. Almost everyone needs a little practice.
- When you're stitching on fabric, use an embroidery hoop. It will help keep your fabric straight, square, and flat.
- The normal motions of stitching often cause the thread to tangle. When your thread becomes twisted, let the needle hang down and dangle freely until the thread unwinds itself. It's a good idea to do this every once in a while, even if you don't think you need to.
- Nobody's perfect! To recover from a bad stitch or two, simply remove the needle from your thread. Then, working from the wrong side of your surface, use the needle to loosen the thread and undo the stitch. Rethread your needle with the same thread, redo the stitch, and get back to work. To correct more than a few bad stitches, use your embroidery scissors to clip the stitches on the wrong side of the surface, taking care not to cut the surface. Use tweezers to pick out the stitches from the right side.

STITCHES

straight stitch

This stitch creates a little dash. Bring the needle up to the right side of the surface at your starting point. Insert the needle the desired distance from the starting point; then pull it to the back of the surface. That's it.

cross-stitch

Cross-stitch is making one diagonal straight stitch across another, with the stitches crossing in the center. For long lines of cross-stitches, work all the diagonal stitches in one direction and then turn around and work the stitches in the other direction. The cross-stitches in this book are free-form, unlike counted cross-stitches that require a chart or special even-weave surface.

zigzag

These straight stitches work all the diagonal stitches in one direction and then turn around and work the stitches in the other direction.

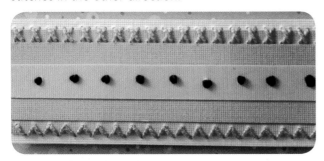

Top to bottom: cross-stitch, zigzag

tip

If you're a lefty and these embroidery stitch illustrations are confusing you, use a computer to reverse them so you'll have a mirror image copy. (Or take them to a copy shop and ask them to make mirror images for you.) Refer to your copies while you're learning new stitches. The mirror images will help you visualize the positioning for your needle and thread.

running stitch

This stitch creates a broken dash-space-dash line. Bring the needle up to the right side of the surface at your starting point. Push and pull the needle up and down through the surface along the pattern line, leaving a space between each stitch. For a consistent look, keep the stitches an even size and tension.

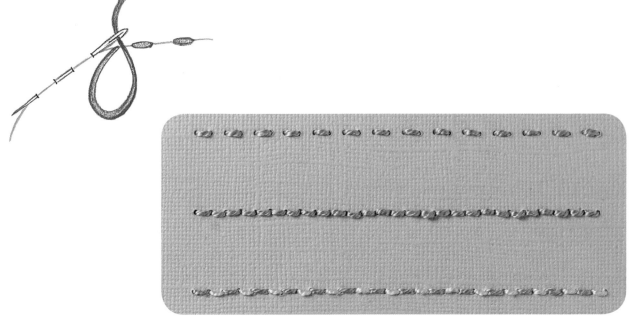

Top to bottom: running stitch, double running stitch, alternating double running stitch

double running stitch

Use this stitch to create a solid line of end-to-end dashes; you can use a different color for each line of stitches to make a solid line of alternating colored dashes. Stitch a line of evenly spaced running stitches. Using the same holes, stitch another row of running stitches, filling in the empty spaces left by the first line of stitches.

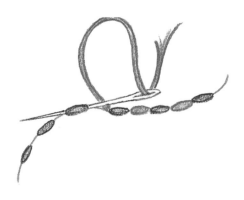

whipped running stitch

This stitch creates a solid, raised, twisted line that looks like a small cord. Make a base line of double running stitches. Begin the whipping step at the starting point of the base row. Use a tapestry needle to lace under a stitch, whip the thread over it, then lace the thread under the following running stitch.

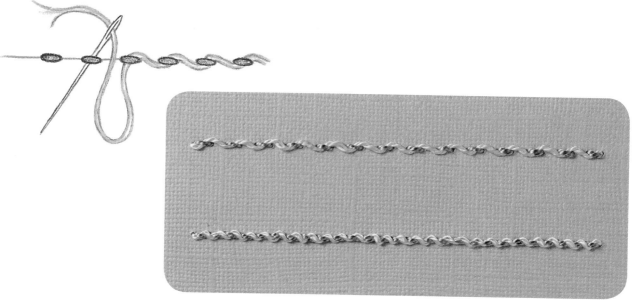

Top to bottom: whipped running stitch, whipped double running stitch

chain stitch

Perfectly named, this stitch looks like a chain! Bring the needle up to the right side of the surface at your starting point. Hold the thread toward you with your free thumb; take a stitch into the same hole where the thread was brought up, forming a small loop. Bring the needle up through the surface where you want the end of the stitch, but do not pull the thread through yet. Bring the needle out and over the loop. Use your free hand to guide the thread around the needle, making a second loop overlapping the first one. Repeat.

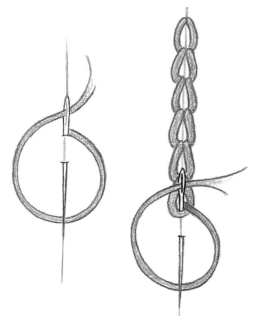

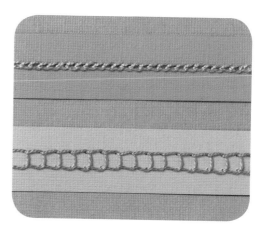

Top to bottom: chain stitch, square chain stitch

square chain stitch

Use this stitch to make a wide "ladder-looking" stitch that can be laced with ribbon or other fibers. Draw two parallel lines where you want to stitch. You'll be stitching downward between the two parallel guidelines. Bring the needle up to the right side of the surface at your starting point on the left line. Insert the needle on the right line, directly across from your starting point; then in the same motion, bring the needle out under the starting point on the left line. *Don't pull the needle through yet. Loop the thread under the needle tip, then pull the thread through, but don't pull the thread tight. Leave a loop that you can insert the needle into to form the next stitch. Insert the needle into the right line, directly across from the emerging thread. Bring your needle up on the left line underneath the emerging thread. Repeat from * to the end of the line.

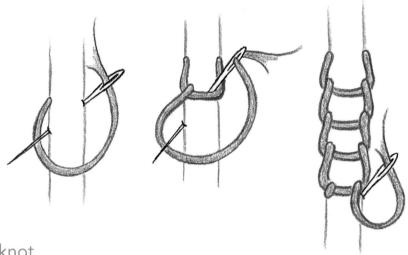

french knot

This raised, round dot looks like a bead. Bring the needle up to the right side of the surface. With your free hand, grip the thread about 2" (5.1 cm) from the spot and pull it taut but not tight. Wind the thread that is between your fingers and the surface around the needle once. Continue holding the thread taut, while inserting the needle back into the starting point hole (or very close to it). Pull the thread through the wound loop and surface to the wrong side. Secure the thread after each French knot. For larger knots, called bullion stitches, wind the thread around the needle two or three times.

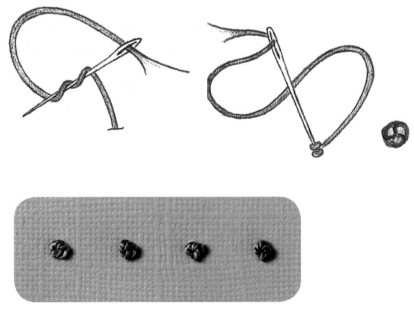

French knot

blanket stitch

This stitch is often used as an embellishment and to secure the edges of appliqués. Insert the needle from the right side of the surface through to the back. Bring the needle up while holding the loop of thread with your left thumb. Make a stitch, bringing the needle out over the loop made by the thread. Pull the needle through until the blanket stitch is snug against the surface.

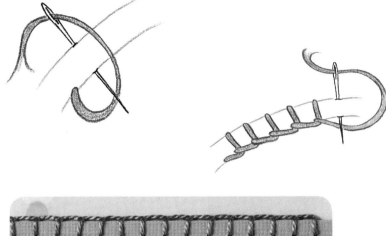

Top to bottom: blanket stitch, knotted blanket stitch

knotted blanket stitch

This looks just like the blanket stitch, but has a tiny knot at each stitch. Working from left to right on the edge of the surface, bring the needle up from the back a bit from the edge and make a blanket stitch. Before moving to the next blanket stitch, loop the needle behind the two threads that hang from the edge of the surface. To keep even tension, you may find it helpful to hold the top of the blanket stitch while you make the knot. Repeat as you would for the blanket stitch, inserting the needle into the right side of the surface and taking the next stitch a bit to the right of the previous stitch.

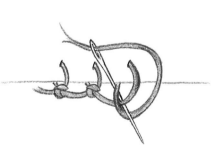

backstitch

Use this stitch to make a solid line of end-to-end dashes. Bring the needle up to the right side of the surface one stitch length from the starting point. Insert the needle at the starting point. Then bring it up again, two stitch lengths away. Pull the thread through, making a stitch. Repeat the first step, inserting your needle at the end of the stitch you just made.

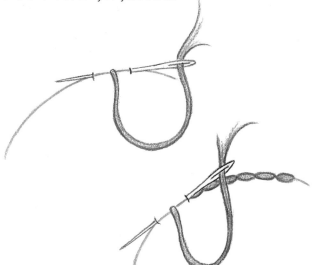

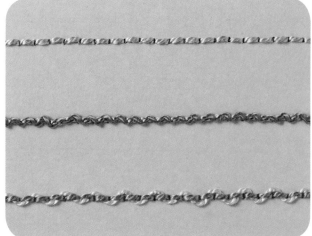

Top to bottom: backstitch, whipped backstitch, woven backstitch

whipped backstitch

This stitch creates a raised, twisted line that looks like a small cord. Make a base line of backstitches. Begin the whipping step at the starting point of the base row. Use a tapestry needle to lace under a backstitch, whip the thread over it, then lace the thread under the following backstitch.

woven backstitch

An extra thread snakes back and forth under backstitches to create this stitch. Stitch a base row of backstitches. Use a tapestry needle to weave under a backstitch from the top to the bottom. Then weave under the following stitch from the bottom to the top.

double woven backstitch

Two extra threads snake back and forth under the backstitches to form this stitch. Stitch a row of woven backstitches. Start a new thread working the same way as the woven backstitch, filling in the empty spaces on the opposite side.

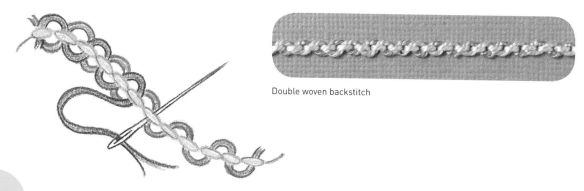

Double woven backstitch

split stitch

This stitch looks like a small tight chain stitch, and it's an easy stitch for outlining letters. Make a small straight stitch. Then bring the needle to the right side again halfway along the stitch you've just made, splitting the thread with the tip of the needle. Repeat to the end of the line.

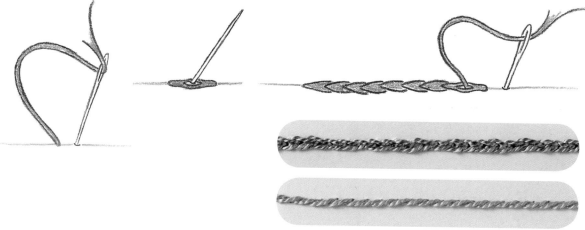

Top to bottom: split stitch, stem stitch

stem stitch

This stitch looks like a narrow twisted cord. Bring the needle up on your pattern line and take a small stitch. Come back up close alongside the last stitch, at about the halfway point of the stitch. Take another stitch and come up alongside it. Repeat to the end of the line.

whipped stem stitch

This stitch looks like a slightly raised cord. Stem stitch a base line. Begin the whipping step at the starting point of the base line. Use a tapestry needle to lace under a stitch, whip the thread over it, then lace the thread under the following stitch.

Pattern Transfer onto Paper or Cardstock

Less is more when it comes to pattern marking. Good practice is to make as few marks as you need and to make them as light as you can. The goal is to have very light guides to show you where to cut, fold, and pierce and to avoid any marks that might show on your finished project.

You can use your computer/home printer to copy, enlarge, or reduce a pattern and print directly onto your crafting paper. Just use the "draft" or "low quality" setting to get a faint pattern that won't bleed through your paper. It's a good idea to print the "mirror image" onto the wrong (back) side of your crafting paper, too.

We hate to admit that this is one of those times when technology really does make life a little easier. But never fear, from the computer savvy to the old-school crafter, we've got you covered. You can try all three of these techniques to see which works best for you.

you'll need

copy machine, scanner,
 or just plain old tracing paper
craft scissors and/or craft knife
pencil
removable tape

easy method: trace and transfer

If you have a copy machine or scanner, make a copy of the pattern on plain copy paper. If not, lay a piece of tracing paper over the pattern and trace the outline and piercing holes with a pencil.

Next, roughly cut around the pattern (leave about a half inch, to be safe) and arrange it on the paper or cardstock that you're going to use for the project. Secure the pattern into place with a couple pieces of removable tape.

Don't have any removable tape on hand? Just press a piece of regular household tape to your clothing a couple times to remove some of its "stick."

tip

Once you've transferred the pattern onto your paper it's time to check the project instructions to see if you're ready to pierce holes:

A: If they don't specify to wait, pierce the holes following the instructions on page 72.

B: If the instructions tells you to pierce holes later in the project, just proceed to the next step and set the pattern piece aside until the instructions tell you to pierce the holes.

you'll need

- light box, window, or a glass tabletop and some good lighting
- craft scissors and/or craft knife
- pencil
- removable tape

easier method: lighten up

This low-tech method only works on light paper. Sorry, no heavy cardstock or super dark colors.

This method is less awkward if you start by carefully trimming the pattern page out of your book. Most authors wouldn't suggest cutting their book apart, but when we can, we like to make things quicker and easier.

Next, use removable tape to stick the paper you'll be using for your project on top of the pattern.

If you have a light box, place the two sheets on top of it, so that the light makes the pattern visible. If you don't have a light box, you can improvise one by using a window or glass tabletop instead. Just make sure there is good light coming through from the back/bottom.

Now all you have to do is use a pencil to trace the pattern and piercing holes right onto the paper.

you'll need

- craft scissors and/or craft knife
- pencil
- removable tape

easiest method: oh, cut it out

Carefully trim the pattern page out the book, cut it out on the pattern, and pierce holes in the pattern.

Now you have a template. Trace around it and mark the piercing holes onto anything you like!

To make a sturdy, reusable template or stencil, use a copy machine or computer/printer to print the pattern onto plain white cardstock and cut it out with craft scissors. Cut any inner shapes using a craft knife and self-healing cutting mat. Tape an envelope to the inside of the cover of your book to store your patterns.

method option:

Are you a download junky? Head to creativepub.com/stitchestemplates to print out the patterns from this book directly onto your paper or cardstock.

working with alphabet patterns

These alphabet patterns offer creative possibilities to make basic cards more personalized. For example, instead of using the bébé bottle design with the picture frame window card, you could stitch "get well" or "merci." You could even stitch an initial on a tag card or stitch a word or phrase wherever there's room.

MAKE IT YOUR OWN!

Here's how to make your own pattern—it's as easy as A B C!

A. Copy the letters. Decide which style has the right flavor for your project. Then use a copy machine to reproduce the letters you need, reducing or enlarging them to the perfect size. Cut out the letters, carefully trimming close to the outlines of the letter patterns.

B. Design the layout. Draw a baseline for your layout on white cardstock or paper. Most times you'll use a ruler to draw a straight line. You can use a compass or trace the shape of something round or oval to draft an arc. Experiment with other layouts as well.

Arrange your cutout letters on the white cardstock. The alphabet patterns have a baseline to help you keep your lettering in a straight line and at a uniform slant. Align the baselines as a guide to line up your letters. You don't stitch the baseline. Aim to keep the spacing between the letters even looking. Sometimes the connecting strokes between letters might need to be adjusted so they look right for your design. Use an ordinary pencil to draw any changes to the letters. When you decide on the placement of the letters, tape the individual letters in place on the cardstock.

C. Make the pattern. Use a copy machine to make a copy of the final layout, or tape a fresh piece of tracing paper over your whole layout and then trace over your design with a fine-tip permanent marker. You've created your own personalized pattern.

Now just transfer the pattern onto your fabric or paper and get stitching!

All of the alphabets in this book, or online, can be backstitched onto paper, cardstock, or fabric. The open spaces in some alphabets can be filled in with paint, chalk, glitter, or even beads. Bubble Graffiti looks great when combined with the paper appliqué technique.

Create uppercase letters easily! Some alphabets have only lowercase (small) letters or only uppercase (capital) letters. When you're using one of these alphabets and you'd ordinarily use a capital letter to start a name or word, use an "initial cap." Just make the initial letter a little bit larger than the other letters.

Here are a few hints for centering lettering in a design. The center of your design is not necessarily the middle of the middle letter. To find the center of your design, just fold the pattern in half, matching the beginning of the first word to the end of the last word. Mark the center fold with a transfer pen or pencil. Then simply match the center of your pattern to the spot on your paper where you want the center of the embroidered design to be.

alphabet patterns

typewriter type-ography

abcdefghijk

lmnopqrstu

vwxyz

happy cursive handwriting

abcdefghi

jklmnopqr

stuvwxyz

bubble graffiti

ABCDEFGHI

JKLMNOPQR

STUVWXYZ

urban gothic

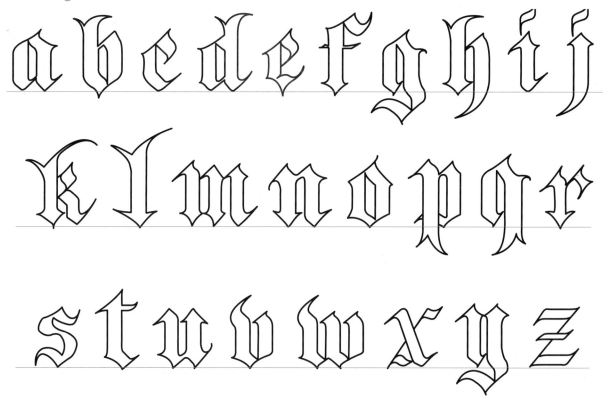

card patterns

Go online at creativepub.com/stitchestemplates to easily print out your patterns on cardstock or paper. Unless noted, all patterns are full size.

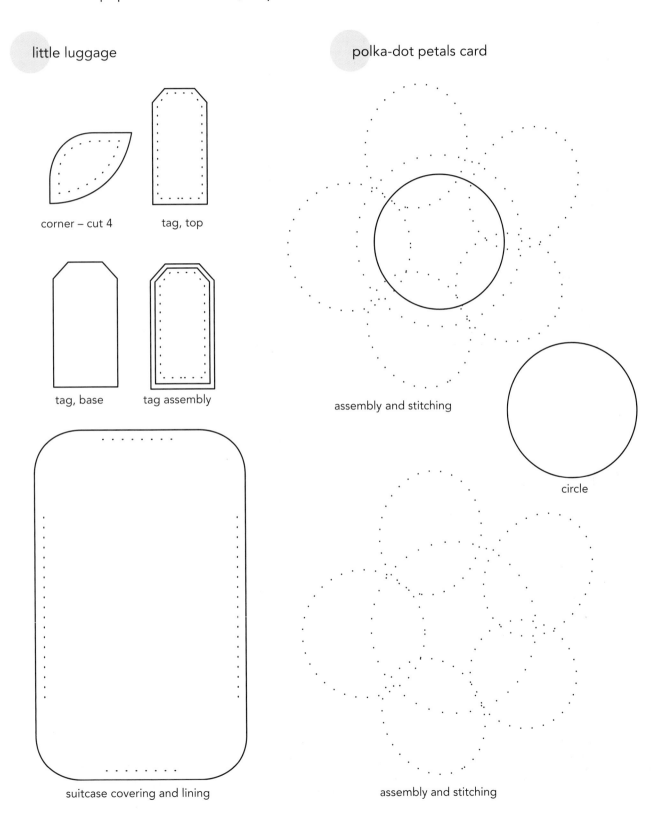

little luggage

corner – cut 4

tag, top

tag, base

tag assembly

suitcase covering and lining

polka-dot petals card

assembly and stitching

circle

assembly and stitching

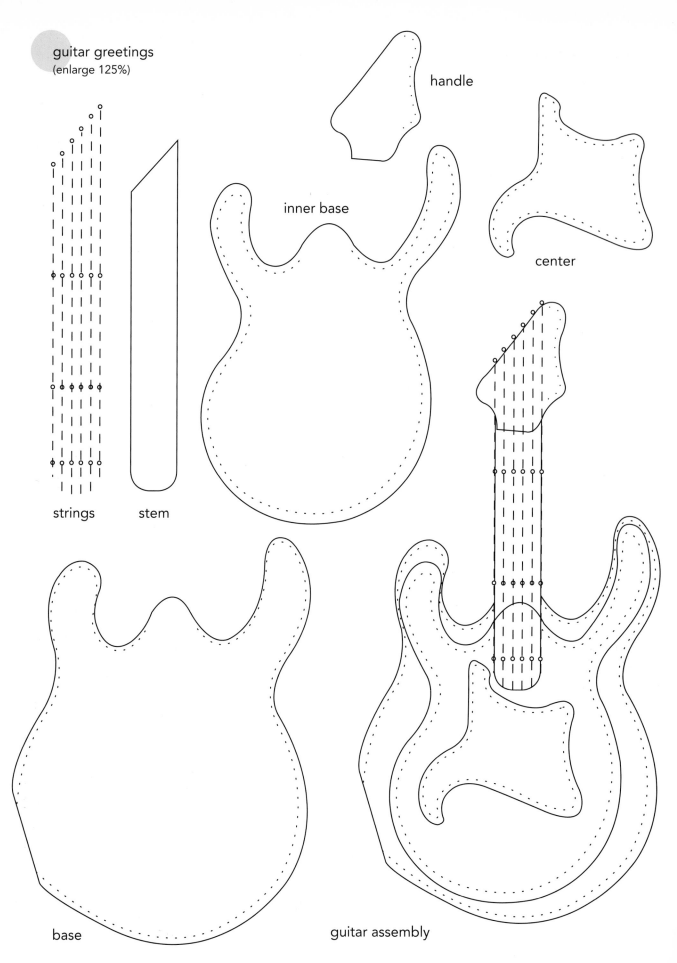

guitar greetings
(enlarge 125%)

handle

inner base

center

strings   stem

base

guitar assembly

hands in harmony mini card

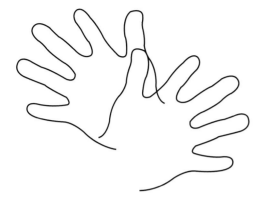

large hands

small hands

cake!

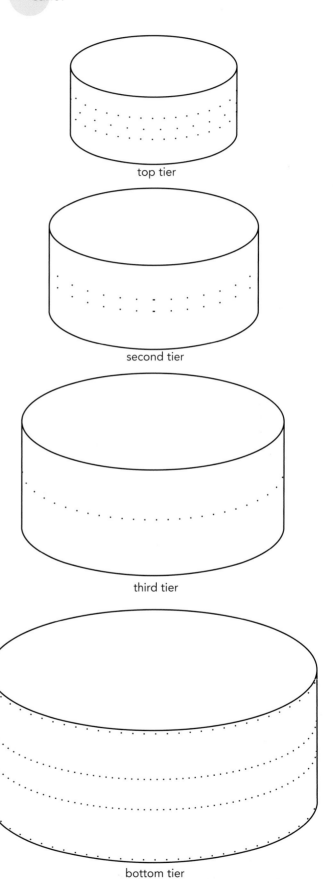

top tier

second tier

third tier

bottom tier

cake!

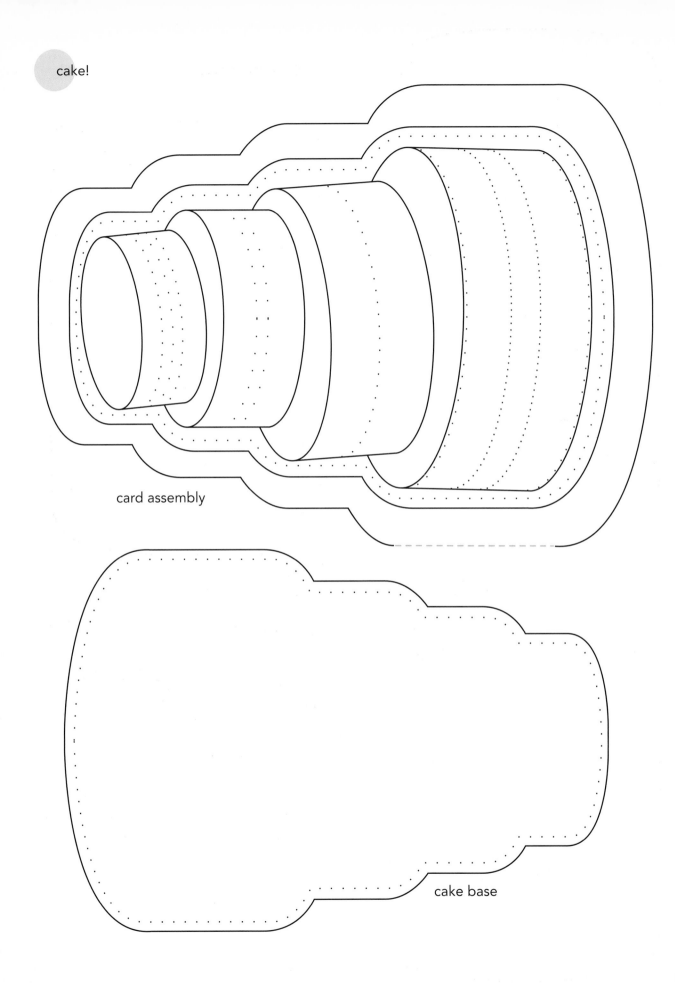

card assembly

cake base

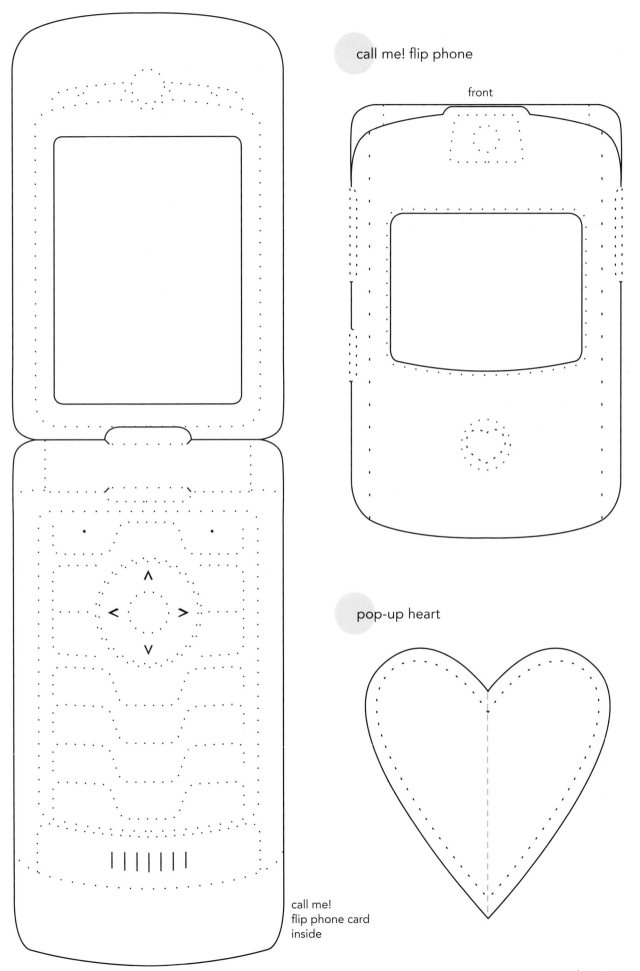

call me! flip phone

front

pop-up heart

call me!
flip phone card
inside

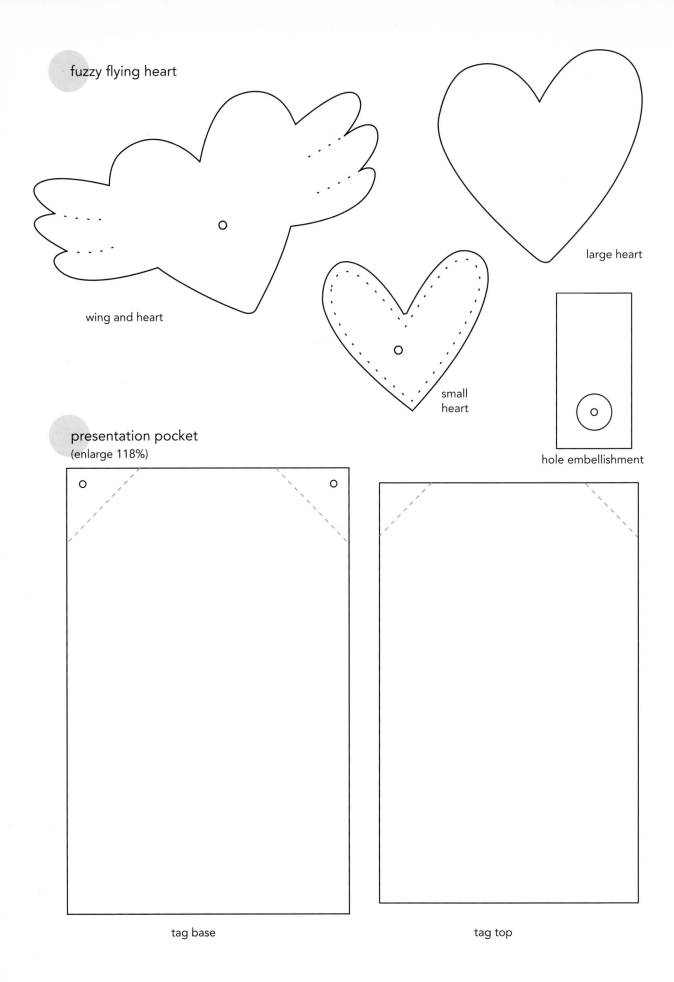

fuzzy flying heart

wing and heart

large heart

small
heart

hole embellishment

presentation pocket
(enlarge 118%)

tag base

tag top

pocket lining

pocket base

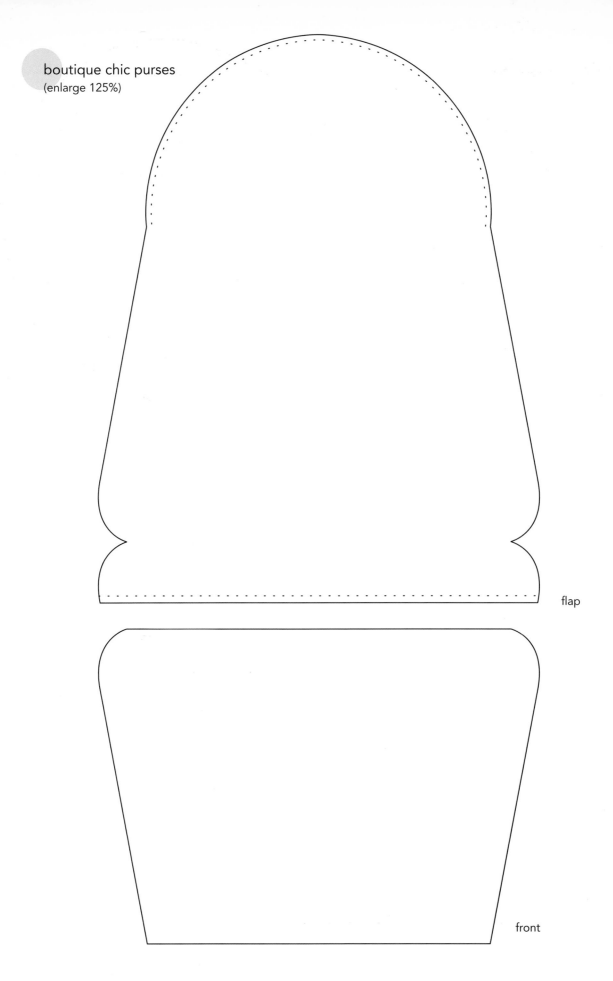

boutique chic purses
(enlarge 125%)

flap

front

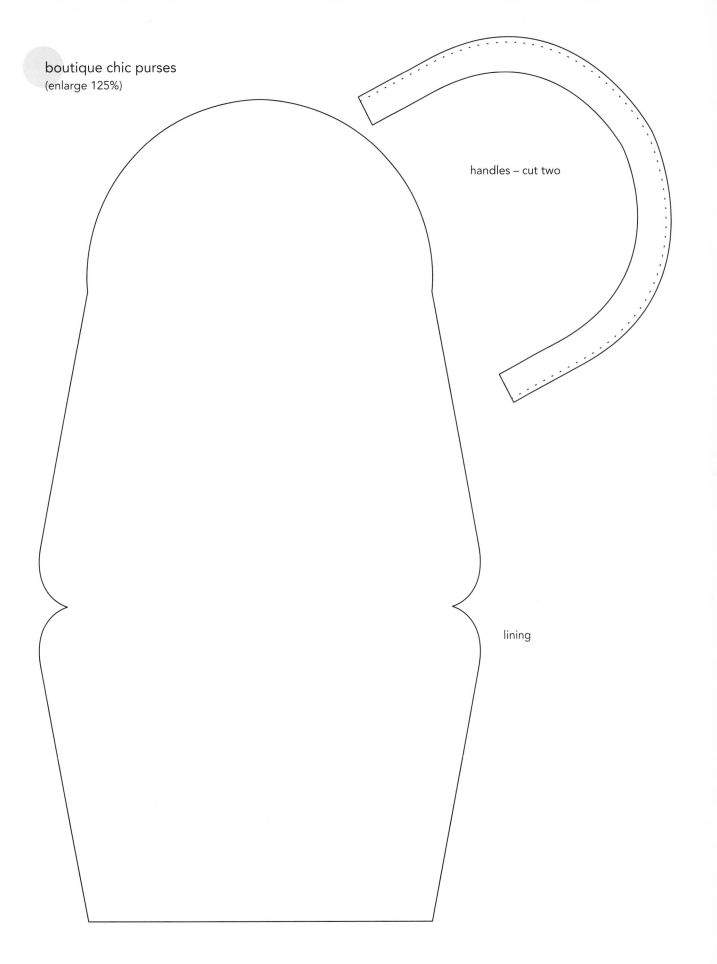

boutique chic purses
(enlarge 125%)

handles – cut two

lining

bébé bottle

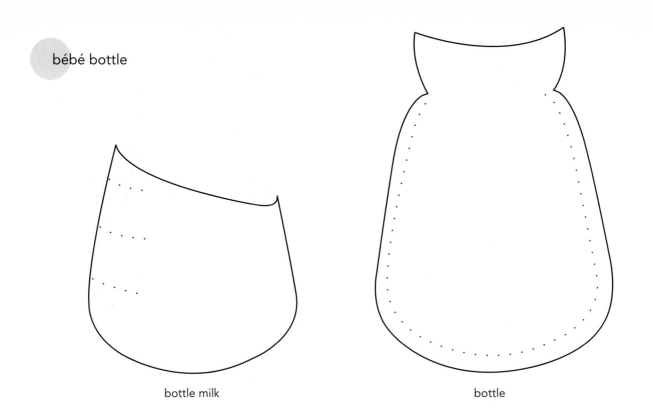

bottle milk

bottle

picture frame card

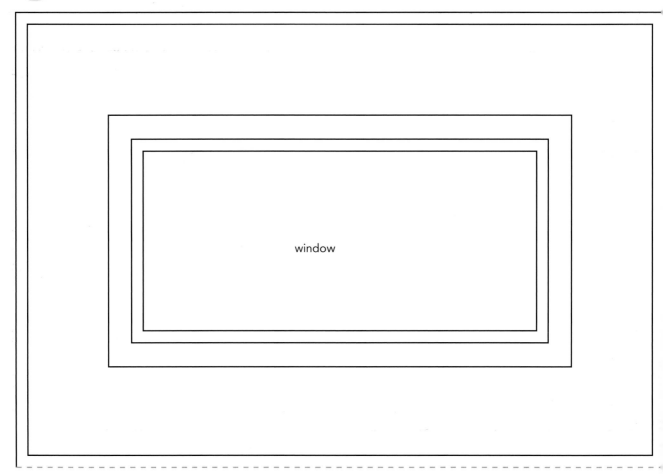

window

front

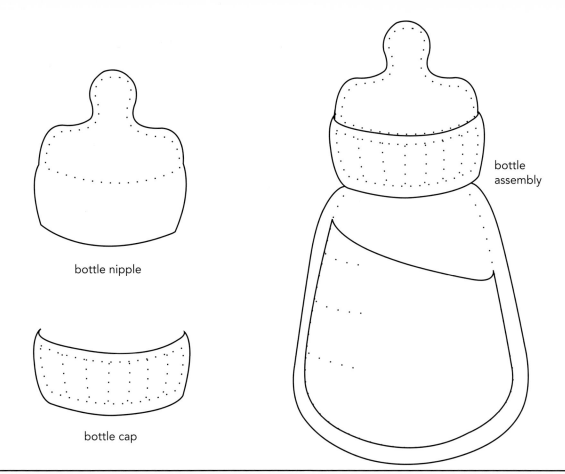

bottle nipple

bottle cap

bottle
assembly

inside

roof, shutters, door, and stitching

key

house

card

assembly

tag topper and tag

cactus cocktail

cactus assembly

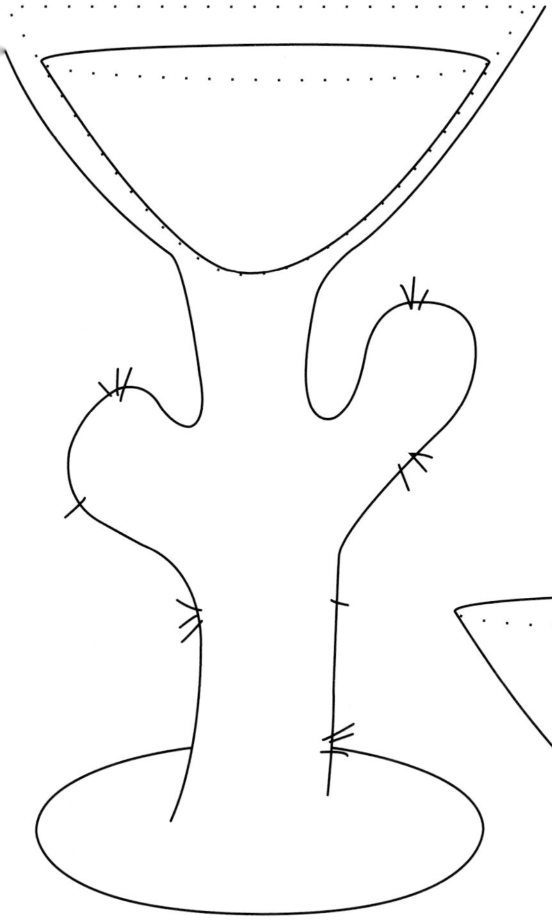

cactus glass and stitching

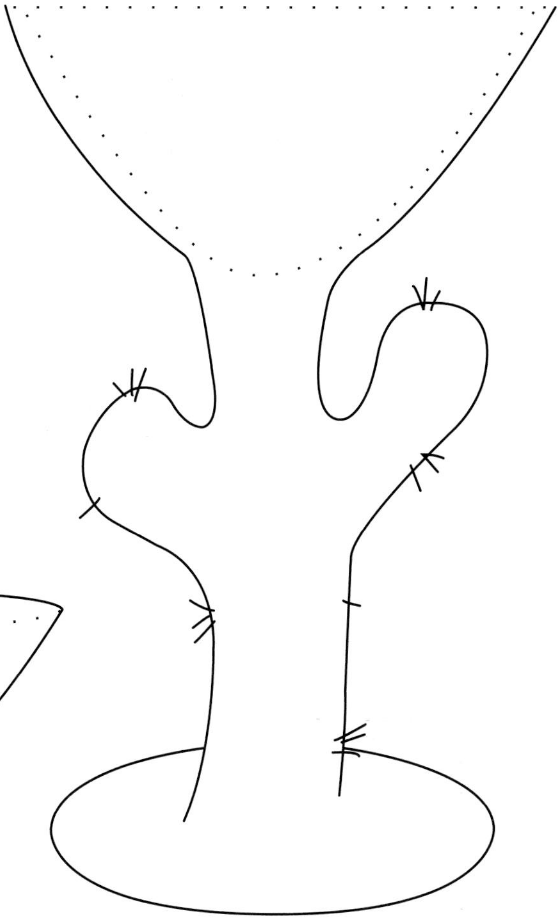

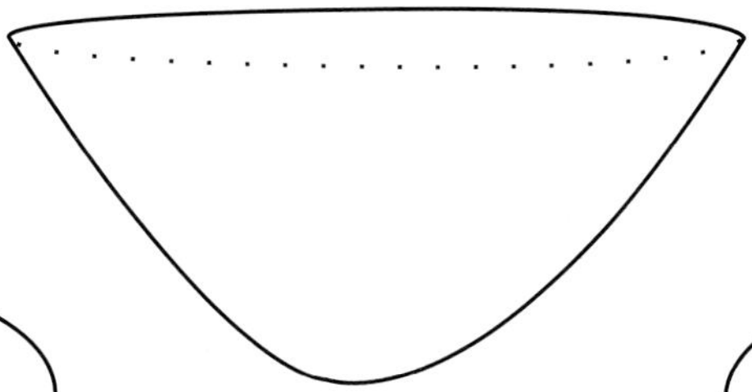

cactus drink

lyrical note iPod
(enlarge 143%)

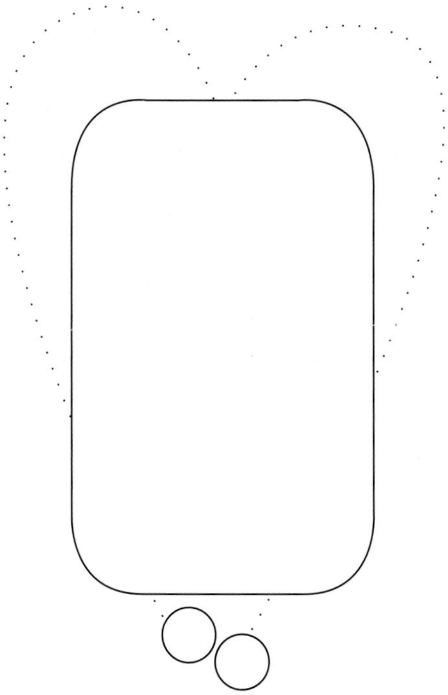

assembly

card

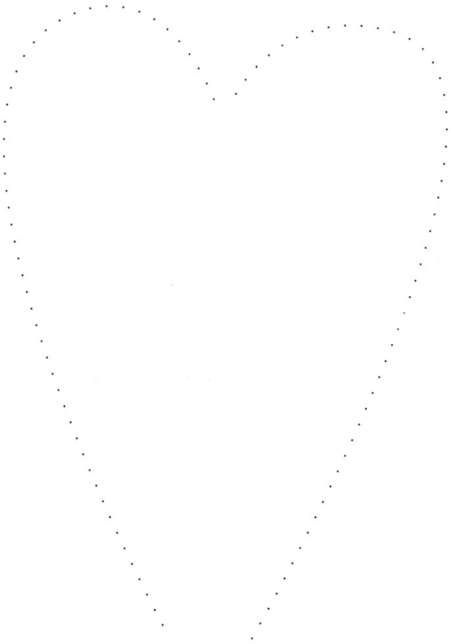

stitching guide

ribbonbird

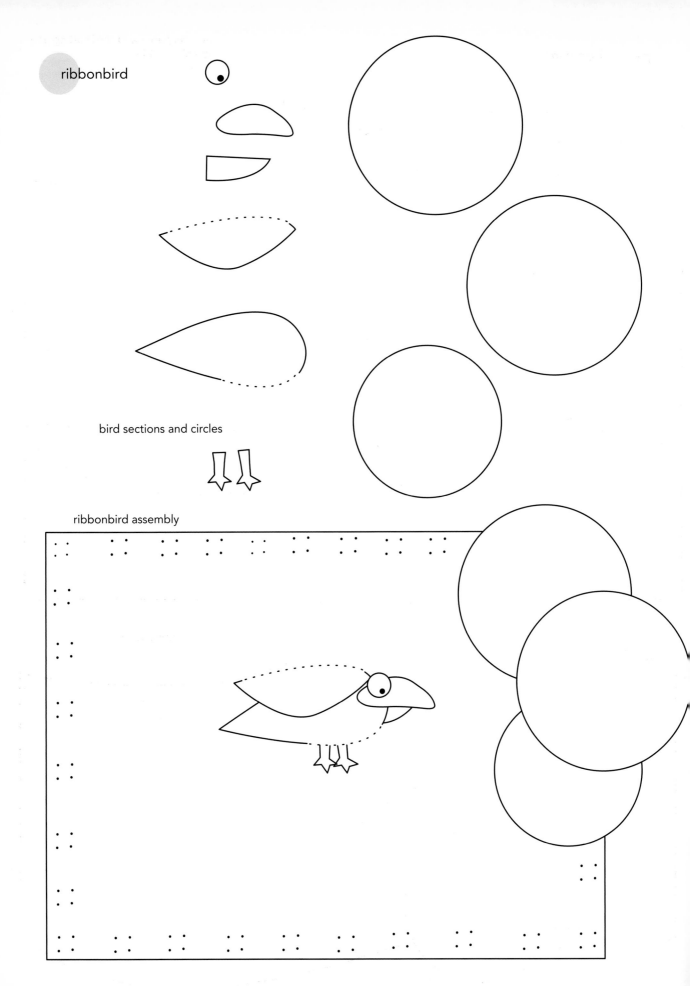

bird sections and circles

ribbonbird assembly

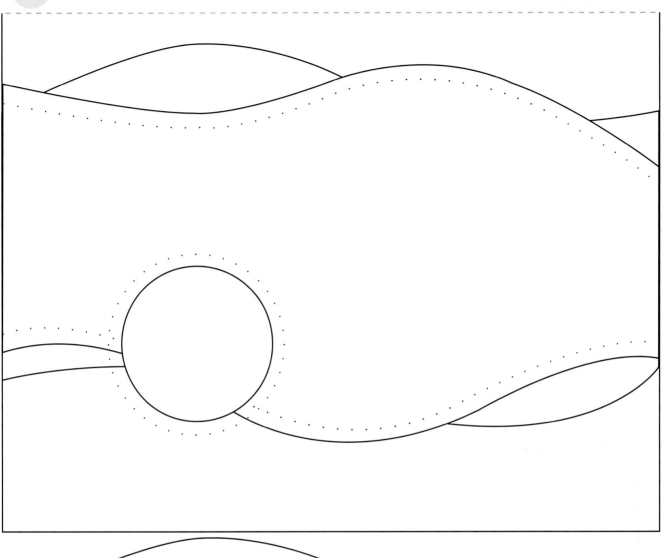

orange print paper

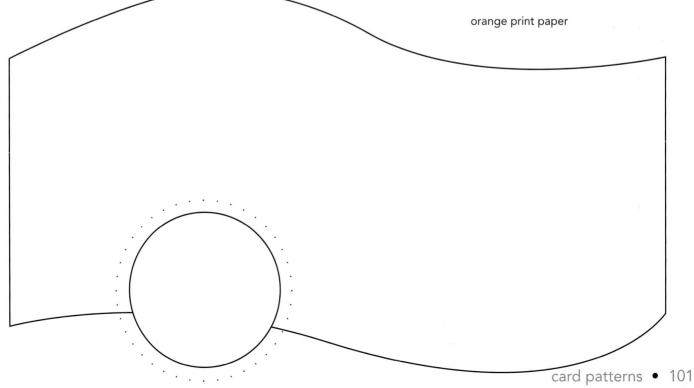

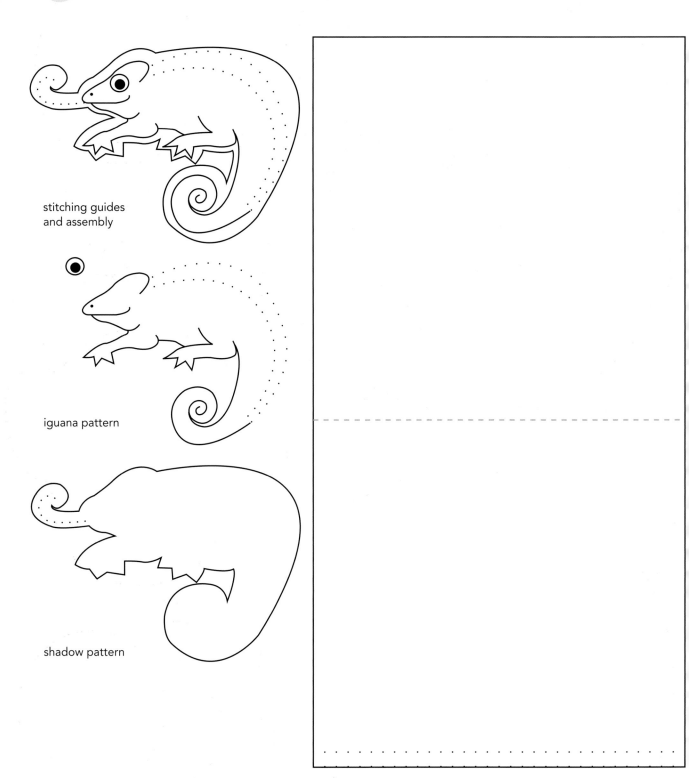

stitching guides
and assembly

iguana pattern

shadow pattern

card

cheeky monkey

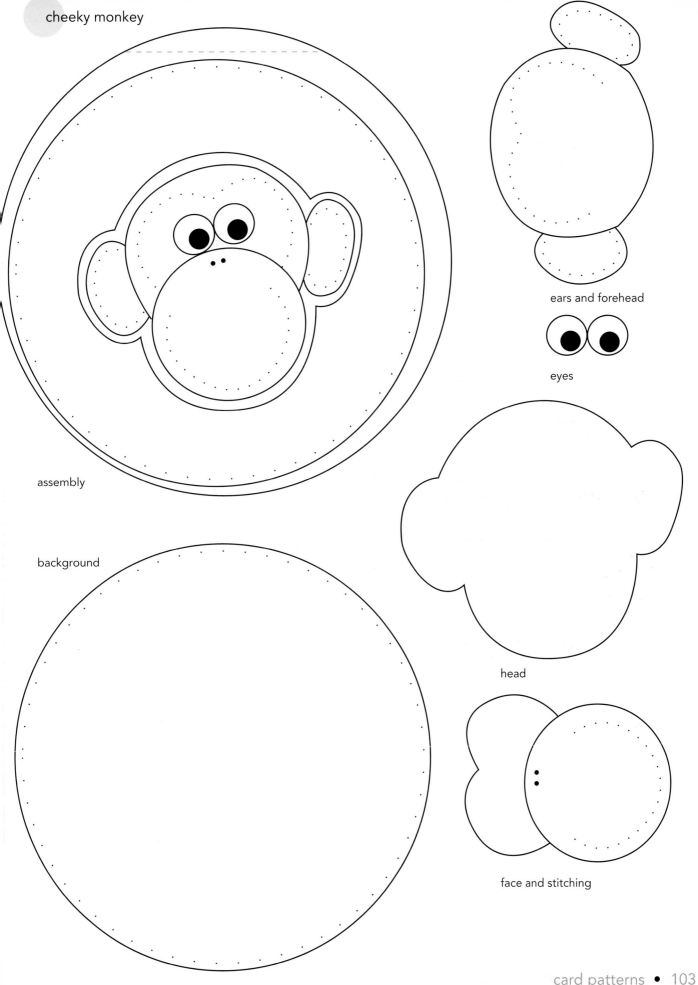

ears and forehead

eyes

assembly

background

head

face and stitching

inside assembly

d.

c.

b.

body

a.

o

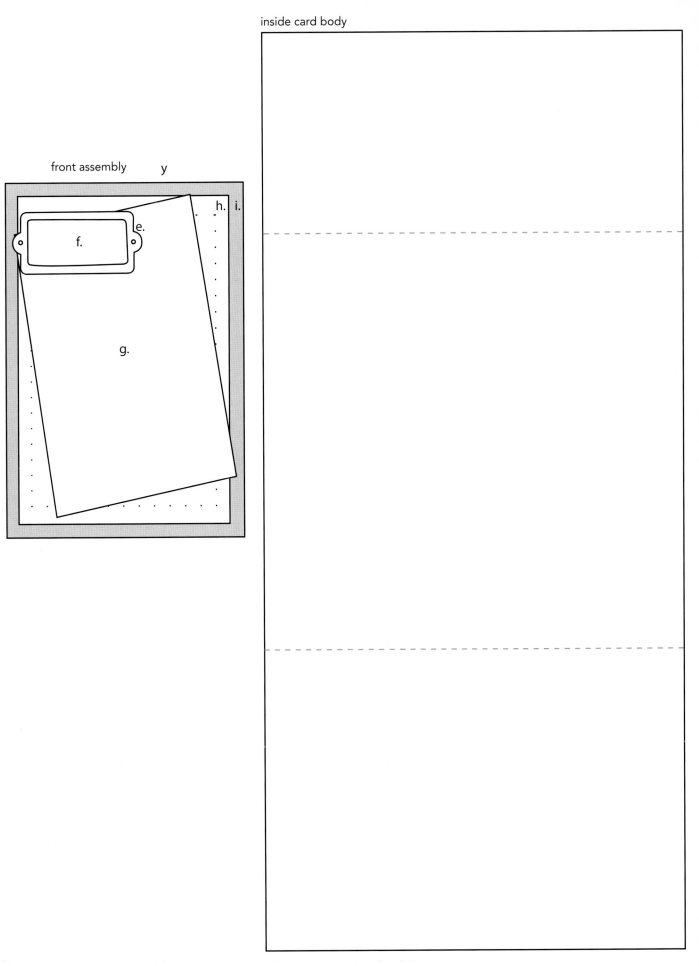

inside card body

front assembly   y

h. i.

e.

f.

g.

gift package two-fold card
(enlarge 125%)

inside pieces

d.

c.

front piece h.

b.

a.

inside pieces

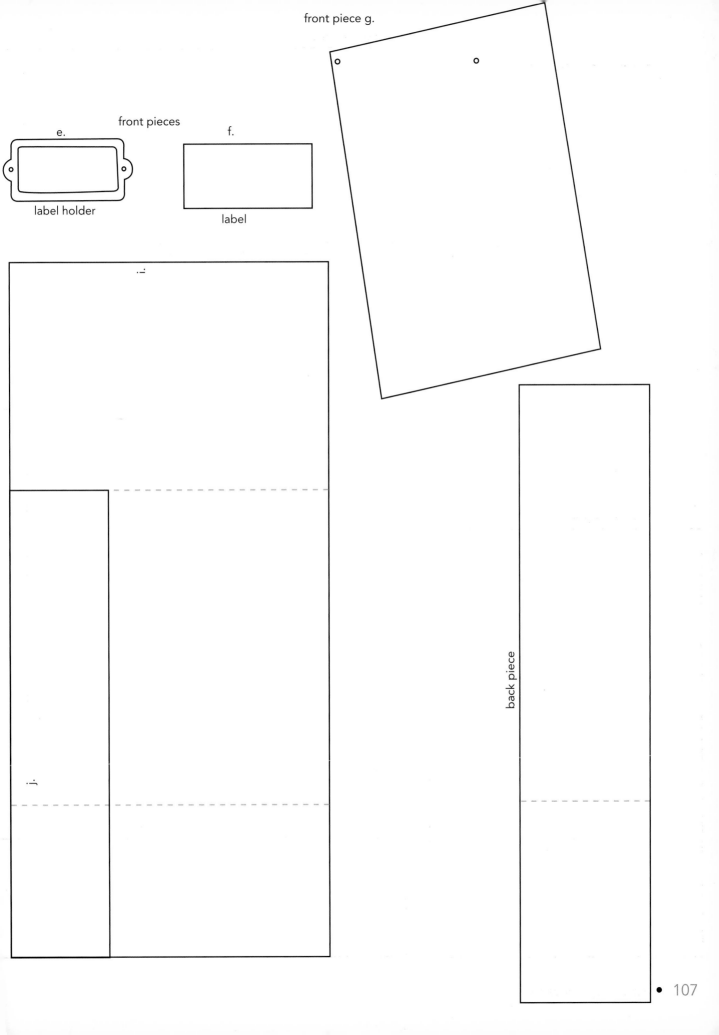

front piece g.

front pieces

e.

f.

label holder

label

i.

j.

back piece

easy envelope template

some alternative top flap suggestions

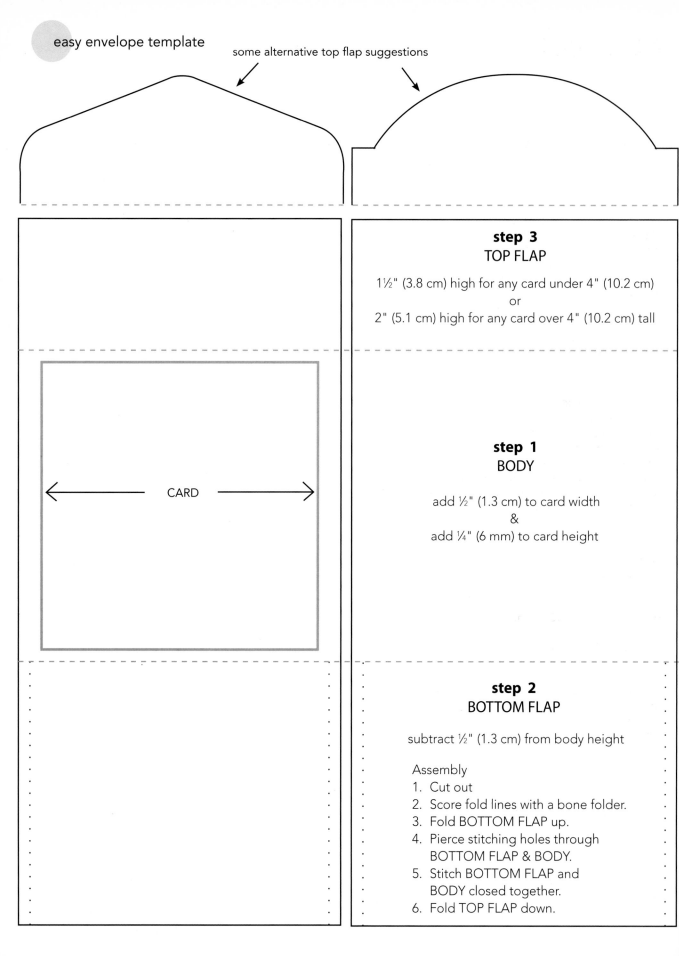

CARD

step 3
TOP FLAP

1½" (3.8 cm) high for any card under 4" (10.2 cm)
or
2" (5.1 cm) high for any card over 4" (10.2 cm) tall

step 1
BODY

add ½" (1.3 cm) to card width
&
add ¼" (6 mm) to card height

step 2
BOTTOM FLAP

subtract ½" (1.3 cm) from body height

Assembly
1. Cut out
2. Score fold lines with a bone folder.
3. Fold BOTTOM FLAP up.
4. Pierce stitching holes through
   BOTTOM FLAP & BODY.
5. Stitch BOTTOM FLAP and
   BODY closed together.
6. Fold TOP FLAP down.

sources

HERE'S WHAT WE USED:

adhesives

tape – SCOTCH, 3M
removable tape – SCOTCH, 3M
glue stick – ELMER'S Craft Bond
jewel glue – api, CRAFTER'S PICK
fabric glue – api, CRAFTER'S PICK
double-sided tape runner – FISKARS
double-sided adhesive foam squares –
    THERM O WEB, peel-n-stick
double-sided tacky tape –
    PROVO CRAFT, Terrifically Tacky Tape
glue dots – GLUE DOTS INT.

tools

needles – THE DMC CORP.
needle threaders – THE DMC CORP.
needle puller – PRYM-DRITZ
shears & scissors – GINGHER, FISKARS
craft knife & self-healing cutting mat – FISKARS
paper trimmer & hole punches – FISKARS
paper piercer – LASTING IMPRESSIONS FOR PAPER INC.
mouse pad – LASTING IMPRESSIONS FOR PAPER INC.

materials

acrylic paints – DELTA, Ceramcoat
thread conditioner – THREAD HEAVEN
tracing paper – STRATHMORE
transfer pen – DMC, Linea, Fabric Marker
transfer pencil – DMC, Linea, White Pencil
iron-on transfer pencil –
    WRIGHTS, Hot-Iron Transfer Pencil
dressmaker's transfer paper –
    SARAL, Wax Free Transfer Paper
transfer mesh – STITCH WITCHERY, Fusible Web
iron-on adhesive, light weight –
    THERM O WEB, Heat n Bond Lite
cardstock – unless otherwise noted – BAZZILL BASICS

Thank you to the wonderful, friendly people at the DMC Corporation, Fiskars Brands, Inc., Petaloo, Creative Crystal Company, Dreamweaver Stencils, Wichelt Imports, Inc., and Mill Hill Beads for providing materials for this book.

supplies

little luggage: "ciao"
DMC embroidery floss: black #310, very dark blue-violet #333
Gartner Studios: Blue Dot Pattern Paper and Blue Solid Paper, hot hues!
Colorbok: twill tape #34666
Making Memories: "Details" Silver Mini Square
K & Company: Marcella, Super Bright Alphabet Dome Stickers #144019
Offray: grosgrain ribbon

little luggage: "bon voyage"
Krylon: spray paint: Make It Suede! textured paint, #1241 Buckskin
Creative Crystal: mini gold studs
Karen Foster: Jewel mini brads
Offray: grosgrain ribbon
Creek Bank Creations: gold label holder, Finishing Touches
K & Company: alphabet letters, Life's Journey, domed typewriter keys, white #557055
The airplane and Eiffel Tower charms are vintage, antique-shop finds from the designers' hoard.

polka-dot petals
Making Memories: Cheeky Embellishment Paper, "dot"
DMC pearl cotton: Black #310, Blue #3750

hands in harmony mini card
Making Memories: BoHo Chic Embellishment Paper: "brocade dot" and "floral stripe"
Amaco: wax metallic finish, Rub 'n Buff: Patina #76364D
DMC metallic and cotton embroidery floss: Light Effects, Precious Metals Silver #E168
Green #909

boho paisley motif
Making Memories: Boho Chic Embellishment Paper, fluer #28350; Cheeky Embellishment Paper, tweed #2835; paisley #28351
DMC pearl cotton: Violet #153, Medium Beige Brown #840, Turquoise #3844

savvy stitched strips
Colorbok: greeting cards and envelopes, mocha, kiwi, peachy
The Scrapbook Wizard: Pink Dot paper, designed by Melissa Shupe
DCWV: canvas textured cardstock, Vanilla, Bright Pink, Light Pink, Blue, Peach
DMC pearl cotton: Very Light Pistachio Green #369, Sky Blue #519, Medium Cranberry #602, Very Light Cranberry #605, Black Brown #3371
Therm O Web: double-sided adhesive foam squares, peel-n-stick
Karen Foster: metal letters, Alpha Charms
Scrapworks: round white frame embellishment

guitar greeting
Making Memories: Boho Chic Embellishment Paper, Box Flower #28350; Cheeky Embellishment Paper, Stripes #28351
DMC pearl cotton: Snow White #B5200, Black #310, Light Topaz #726, Blue-violet #3838

call me! flip phone
DMC pearl cotton: Black #310, Dark Rose #335, Light Violet #554, Ultra Very Light Dusty Rose #963

pop-up heart
DMC pearl cotton: Very Light Sky #747, Very Light Sky Blue #747, Bubble Gum Pink #3806, Light Cyclamen Pink #3806
Lasting Impressions for Paper, Inc.: papers
Doodlebug Design Inc.: Dot print paper by Cynthia Sandoval
Colorbok: Card & envelope

cake!
Colorbok: Accent Paper Pack 37923, Polka Dot, Blue, Striped, Asterisk, Gradient
DMC Pearl Cotton: Light Tangerine #742, Peacock Blue #807, Snow White #B5200

fuzzy flying heart tag
DMC pearl cotton: Strawberry #776, Medium Pink #726, Lemon Pearl Cotton #727, Very Light Topaz #727, Sky Blue #519

versatile tag card
Lasting Impressions for Paper, Inc.: Lilac, Yellow Dot Print cardstock
DCWV: peachy pink textured cardstock
Frances Meyer, Inc.: pink dot print paper
Chatterbox: mini brads
Offray: ribbon

perfect presentation pocket
Frances Meyer, Inc.: Pink Dot paper
DCWV: Peachy Pink cardstock
Fiskars: scalloped edge craft scissors
DMC embroidery floss: Bubble Gum Pink #3806, Medium Antique Mauve #316
Chatterbox: mini brads
Krylon: spray paint, Whitewash
Making Memories: label holder
Offray: ribbon

boutique chic purses

DMC pearl cotton: Strawberry #3354, Light Dusty Rose #3716
DCWW paper: Stripe, Chocolate Flower & Paisley Print, Dot Print
Lasting Impressions for Paper, Inc.: cardstock
Velcro: round self-adhesive fasteners
Karen Foster: jewel mini brads
Fiskars: hole punch
Chatter Box: snap-on fasteners, Scrapbook Interiors
Petaloo: self-adhesive flower, Regal International
Foofala: metal clasp, Knockers
Making Memories: silver brads
Boutique Trims, Inc.: lock & key charms, Embellish It!
Crafts Etc!: ribbon
Trims & Buttons, Inc.: itsy-bitsy buttons
Mill Hill: beads
Creative Crystal: nail heads, stars, and Swarovsky crystals

bébé bottle picture frame card

DMC embroidery floss: Light Lavender #211, Very Light Cranberry #605, Ultra Very Light Baby Blue #3756
Lasting Impressions for Paper, Inc.: Light Pink, Lavender, Lime Sherbet cardstocks
Joann Fabrics: clear lightweight vinyl
Doodlebug Design Inc.: Fruit Hoops paper
DCWV: textured, Bubble Gum Pink cardstock
Offray: ribbon
Noteworthy: heart charm, Simply Beading

key to a happy home

Colorbok: Love cards & envelopes #37967
Making Memories: Boho Chic Embellishment Paper #28350, Floral Stripe
DMC pearl cotton: Light Violet #554, Chartreuse #703, Very Light Topaz #727, Ultra Dark Coffee Brown #938, Ultra Very Light Dusty Rose #963

cactus cocktail

DMC pearl cotton: Light Lemon #445, Chartreuse #703

lyrical note iPod

DMC pearl cotton: white #Blanc
Colorbok: card
DCWV: music print, stripe, dot print papers
Chatterbox: swirl print paper
Making Memories: tags
K & Company: dome letter stickers

i wanna iguana

Making Memories: Cheeky Embellishment Paper, Flower #28351
DMC pearl cotton: Rose #335; Tangerine, Light #742; Royal

Blue, Dark, Ultra Dark #796

ribbonbird

DMC embroidery floss: Black #310, Very Dark Royal Blue #820, Burnt Orange #947
Offray: ribbons
Mill Hill: bead
K & Company: Marcella tag

peek-a-boo surprise card

DMC pearl cotton: Very Light Brown #435, Medium Pine Green #3363
Ivy Cottage: tropical foliage print paper, Creative Imaginations by Debbie Mumm
Lasting Impressions For Paper, Inc.: kiwi striped print, blue cardstocks, bright blue textured cardstock
Offray: ribbons

cheeky monkey

Making Memories: Cheeky Embellishment Paper #28351, word
DMC pearl cotton: Coral #351, Light Violet #554, Ultra Dark Coffee Brown #938

gift package

Dreamweaver: gift package stencil, #LL 466
Lasting Impressions For Paper Inc.: light blue cardstock
DMC embroidery floss: Very Light Cranberry #605, Very Light Terra Cotta #758
Chatterbox: flowered print/solid reversible paper; tangerine mini brad, scrapbook tacks

label

DMC embroidery floss: Very Light Cranberry #605
Chatterbox: dark butter reversible cardstock
Doodlebug Design Inc.: bubble blue mini brads, dotlets

cutout flower tag

Chatterbox: flowered print/peach reversible paper; tangerine, rosy and white mini brads, scrapbook tacks
Offray: ribbon
Doodlebug Design Inc.: bubble blue mini brads, dotlets
Making Memories: metal rimmed vellum circle tag

two-fold card

DMC pearl cotton: Very Light Mahogany #402
Chatterbox: flowered print/peach reversible paper, dark butter reversible cardstock, blue dot print paper; rosy mini brad, scrapbook tacks
Offray: grosgrain

Also Available From
Creative Publishing International

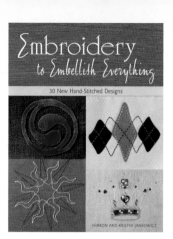

Embroidery to Embellish Everyth
30 new hand-stitched designs
By Sharon and Kristin Jankowicz
ISBN: 1-58923-254-2

To purchase these or other Creative Publishing International titles, contact your local bookseller, or visit our website at www.creativepub.com

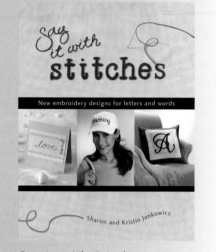

Say It with Stitches
New embroidery designs for letters and words
By Sharon and Kristin Jankowicz
ISBN: 1-58923-270-4

Favors with Flair
75 easy designs for weddings, parties, and events
By Mary Lynn Maloney
ISBN: 1-58923-208-9

Creative Publishing international

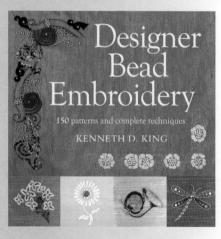

Designer Bead Embroidery
150 patterns and complete techniques
By Kenneth D. King
ISBN: 1-58923-272-0

New Punchneedle Embroidery
Basics & finishing techniques
By Charlotte Dudney
ISBN: 1-58923-299-2